Poems for Longevity, Life Extension, and Rejuvenation

Bob Guth

Table of Contents

Forward

This present volume is basically a rewrite of an earlier book of poems that was entitled, "Poems for Living Longer and Popping Out of the Aging Box." So much new information on how to extend your life has come out since the earlier volume was published that I thought it necessary to add the new material and in doing so, it became obvious that the old title simply did not fit and so this new book of verse has a new title.

One of the biggest changes is in the chapter on life extension that has a whole new section that I called "Life Extension's Modus Operandi." In it there many very powerful energy exercises and meditations that the life extension student should find very helpful. Also added are many new poems, including a poem on the long-fast, and a poem that informs the reader that the basic design of the human body is to live over 200 years. And another new poem looks at how humans create the ills that afflict them. And I added poems on youthing, sexuality and becoming a master.

Like Lord Byron, John Masefield, Thomas Hardy, Robert Frost and many, many other poets of yesteryear, I like rhyme. It is a real craft to be a good rhyme smith and most of today's poetry is not oriented toward rhyme. I would like to see rhyme come back and again be embraced by the poets of today and tomorrow.

Additionally, I feel that for some, the ideas in this book on longevity and life extension may be better accepted in rhyme than they would be in a document or text with many references to authority figures, etc. The idea of living twice as long as humans currently do is hard to accept for most people because today nobody lives that long. But when these ideas are read in poem and verse it may be a little easier for them to be accepted.

Included in this volume is everything I am aware of in the way of practices, processes, techniques, and procedures that can be used to attain longevity and life extension. The reader is encouraged, nay challenged even, to do all of them to the best of their ability to get the most out of this book and receive the greatest benefit from it. I challenge you now, the reader, to go for your own longevity, to extend your life, and to decree that this is going to be the new path for you.

And last, I ask you, how far are you willing to go to allow you own natural longevity to unfold? What are you willing to do to extend your life? How much work are you willing to put into it to make it to 110 years? Are you willing to push it out and go for 140? How about going for 170? And let's go for the gold - how many of you are willing to go for 200 years?

Prologue

May this little book of verse of mine
Nudge beliefs long entrenched in time
With lines that rhyme about how long you can live
For you see, I think that the timing is right to give
Attentive thought about how long a human can live
And make a leap to reach a much longer lifespan
And jump over the short life (the programmed plan).

Asleep now are humans to this idea of longer lives.
I want to awaken mankind to the idea of far greater heights
Of longevity – it's positively becoming possible now --
Days and nights and years and decades of life extension
The birthright of human kind—this I bring to your attention.
You can read how to do this in my book of poetic screed
And for some, its wisdom they may apply and use and heed
For it can seed them for their own longevity.
My little book of longevity verse seeks to disperse
Wisdom as a lexicon of longevity of sorts in poem.

But for others – the doubting Thomas's
They may as well roam the unknowns
Of this great universe to search and seek
Other ways to extend their days, but I doubt if much
Difference will be found for longevity's ways are such
That they always touch on the universal golden rules
And knowing this, these rules can become wisdom's tools
For longevity schools to lead mankind back to the very long lives
Of Methuselah's Day – and now a new brotherhood thrives --
More harmonious relationships – in husbands and wives –
And when numerology's higher master numbers are known –
The master number numbers of forty-four and fifty-five
Warfare will not then be the way – mankind will despise
Forceful conflict – it will end – and then lifespans will really soar –
Mankind will reach the legendary nine hundred years once more!

Chapter 1, Poems for Longevity

What If You Live Two Hundred Years?

What if you knew
That you were going to
Live two hundred years!
What would you do?

What if you knew
That you could master the art
Of immortality and keep yourself apart
From the aging and decrepitude and decay
That is the hallmark of humanity today?
What would you do?

What if you know
That rejuvenation was coming?
Rejuvenation machines forthcoming
Rejuvenation choirs a 'humming
Rejuvenation musicians a 'strumming
Rejuvenation celebrations a 'drumming
What would you do?

What if your future self
Is calling to you
To give you a message from its point of view
That two hundred years in the future of you –
That you're still alive and well?
What would you do?

What if you knew
That you were going to
Live two hundred years!
What would you do?

Your Body Is Designed to Live Over 200 Years

Did you know that your human body is designed
        to live over 200 years?
Can you believe it?

Not now probably, but futurist say in that 10 generations
        we will live that long –
Can you conceive it?

The blueprint of your body is to let you live more
        than twice as long as you do now.
Yogi Masters have demonstrated it – some have lived
        longer – this they will avow.
So, why don't you live that long now?

Well, your thoughts play a big part of it.
        You don't expect it –
and your thoughts tend to manifest whatever you expect.
        That's at the heart of it.
But dozens of others things are involved, and each
        has a role, and all take a toll.
Your world has many toxins (in food, air, and water)
        as reported in any ecosystem poll.
And the DNA in each and every one of your body's cells has a clock,
        and when all those clocks strike the same hour
(Of your maturity) they trigger the death hormone
        release which gets bigger and more powerful with
Each passing year and lock in aging.

And next, all of your life long traumas from fear
        cause soul fragmentation engaging –
Your major organs – thousands happen as you age
        throughout the pages of your life.
Each soul loss cuts off some soul energy
        that your vital organs need –

Great fear cuts off a soul fragment like a knife
        causing you to age.

Also, your DNA is only at one third of its
        potential efficiency, and as such,
It does not allow very much cell repair or
        tissue regeneration, but when
Humanity moves into greater benevolence
        for all peoples and for every nation,
Then it will increase and greatly expand the
        human population's longevity expectation.

And so, it is important to for you to know that your
        human body was very carefully designed
To let you live several hundred years – this exists –
        you can extend your life and maintain it.

This ability is latent now – it is waiting for you to
        evolve out of the dark ages and claim it.
For when human consciousness evolves to much
        higher levels and abhors barbaric war –
Then lifespans will really soar and humans will
        begin living well over 200 years and more.

How Long Do You Think You'll Live?

To J. Nguyen and D. Bennett, 2015

I spoke about a book
Of poems, many on death
A subject I simply cannot brook
For life is everywhere I see and look
It's clear and dear and in my breath.

The author's bio revealed
She died young as you must
If your focus on death is thrust
Her thoughts became congealed
And sealed into the earth and dust.

A neighbor eyed me askance.
She'd overheard my little talk.
"How long do you think you'll live?"
She asked with a loaded glance
Expecting me to cringe and balk.

Her question was a loaded snare
Implying that to belie the norm
Would cast a doubt: beware, beware!
You must, you see, conform.
It said you must comply
With what society says hereby
On how long you can live.
The right response you must supply
And please do not misapply,
But to me it was a battle cry
And so below, I did reply
But, beware, indeed it was a dare.

To some degree, I offered this repartee:
There are those who can foresee
The future long before its infancy
Of submarines that run beneath the sea

And lunar trips a century before the reality.
There are those working upon
Ways to lengthen your life
And man learns anon
The science of living long
And puts an end to war and strife.

Her neighbor said, "Could be!"
"Where do I sign up?" said he.

I looked her right in her eyes
"Eight hundred years!" I replied.
She laughed with great surprise,
Laughed and slapped her thighs,
A challenge for me to teach the wise.

Her neighbor, he identifies
With members of his peers
Who ride and race the bicycle
And extend their lives by many years.
As he is one of them and they
Expect to live longer than the norm
So, he expects a longer stay and aging to keep away
And that is how extended lives are born.

The woman, she identifies
But now it's with the norm
The struggle of the human game
With those who wear the human form
She thinks that man must live and die
With span of life that must conform
To the mass consensus reality norm.

Well, what is the natural span of the life of man?
What are the normal numbers of his years?
From the higher spheres came wisdom to my ears:
The natural span of the life of man is 147 years.
But man does not live anywhere near that long
Half of his potential has been his sorry song.

He does not attain all of the years his linage can
Or even come close to the natural span of man.
Imbalances come and take his natural longevity away
And then imperfections create for him a shorter stay.

There is the tale of a British colonel who was very
Old with a cane and a stooped back and gray hair
Who heard talk of ageless lamas living in a lamasery.
A Fountain of Youth, it seemed to him, and it drew him there.
Two years he lived among them and adapted to their ways
Of peacefulness, clean mountain air, and raw foods,
Rites of rejuvenation, meditation, and mellow moods.

He looked at himself in a mirror and found to his amaze
That his aging had reversed after a dozen score of days!

Wikipedia has many articles on those living long
Twenty-one World War I survivors lived to 105.
Other lists of 114-year-olds still going strong
And even those who claimed 130 before they died.

In a dream, a voice spoke soft and low and clear
And said that man can extend too even more
To lifetimes four
To fifteen score
To three hundred years and even more
Immortality could then be knocking at the door!

But then the voice said that at this time
Negative thoughts and emotions out of rhyme

Continuing struggles with violence and crime
Create cloudy curtains in the current clime
And obscure visions of a longer lifetime.

Let it be – let us talk now of immortality
And challenge the mass belief reality.
It is time for all of you to know
That short lives are programmed so.
Many masters challenge this and go
Far beyond the bounds of human vanity.
They shun thoughts of aging like insanity.
They know that thoughts are creation.
Thoughts are a spider's web that's spun.
Thoughts form the foundation of creation.
Thoughts manifest, each and every one.
The masters see themselves as youthful lads and lasses.
They hold not patterned thoughts of aging like the masses.

And life extension can be an immortality of sorts.
Its rites and rules and rituals can be written as reports
Let us ask then what secrets might there be,
Can mortal man learn to use them like you and me?

The masters say that life extension is in the learning,
That if you do not expect to age, you will not age,
But you have set up a program to age that is burning.
You can release this program and rip up that page to age
If you are able to not get caught up in
The beliefs that you were brought up in.

It is learning how to handle light.
It is an ending of the Draconian night.
It is moving closer to the Creator's love.
It is raising your vibration higher as above.
It is harnessing the great healer called oxygen
It is implementing cell regeneration deep within

It is working with the pranayama breathing rhythm
It is adding light to transform the body with precision
It is utilizing the long-fast to rid age causing senescent cells
It is emerging rejuvenated after this – as the master tells
It is becoming your own healer to keep your health
It is adding healing meditation – this is real wealth.
It is beginning to purge yourself from your own death urge.
It is going to concerts, shows and operas to let joy purge.
It is being kinder and more loving to your peers and others.
It is higher consciousness – treating all as sisters and brothers.
It is choosing to move towards a raw food primal diet.
It is a very healing diet and there are those who swear by it.
It is living in comfort and fun with a life of flowing ease.
It is moving forward without the fear of disease.
It is releasing the aging program and having fun.
It is knowing that much releasing must be done.
It is moving into a much greater joy and bliss.
It is maintaining impeccability in all of this.

Let us speak again about life extension.
If you want it
Desire it
Intend it
Decree it
Expect it
And allow it

Then it must be, it will happen, do you see?
But it must make sense.
You must keep yourself in good health.
You cannot toss poor health over the fence.
You must treasure health for it is real wealth,
You cannot be sickly and expect it to be, do you see?

And you must believe it is possible and you can attain it.
And you must believe you deserve it and can claim it.

It will be possible when your beliefs can sustain it.
You will deserve it when you remove guilt and don't retain it.

If you think it is impossible, it is.
If you think it could be, it will.
If you think you don't deserve it, you won't,
But you may have it still
If you turn those two around
Allowing the potentials to be found.
Nothing is impossible, you see.
The Creator created this universe to be
Unlimited in creativity for you and me.
You deserve all that you can conceive of
Because you were created by God with love.

In the beginning, there will be those
Who can extend their lives by wisdom linking.
Many will say, "He is a thought manifester."
Many will say, "She is a thought manifester."
They can extend their lives by thinking.

If you can learn to utilize the, 'power of the mind'
When all about you fear that power and call it, 'the occult,'
If you can claim that, 'power of the mind,' then you may find
That it can launch you into an extended lifespan like a catapult.

If you can picture and see yourself as perennially young
While everyone about you thinks that you must grow old,
If you can create thoughts and words from mind and tongue
Of youthfulness, then you will let the youthful you within unfold.

If you can go forward in life without the fear of disease
While all around you, the multitudes fear the major ills,
If you can learn the prevention or cure of disease and live in ease,
Then you can go forward in life with no need for medicines or pills.

If you can choose to eat and drink only foods of purity
While others consume fat, sugar, meat and wine,
If you can refine and continually purify your diet, then most assuredly,
You will regenerate yourself, and they will move into an early decline.

If you can shun addictions that attempt to tempt you
While your soul brothers and sisters fall prey to the same,
If you can shut out the addictive substances that corrupt you,
Then you can climb longevity's heights the fallen ones cannot attain.

If you can evolve into higher consciousness and never again say
An unkind word or do an unkind deed to your fellow man,
While all about you, others harm one another in a righteous way,
Then you will heal your heart, mind, emotions and soul
As only one who attains a higher consciousness can.

If the twelve universal laws you can come to know and learn
That interact with humanity – the unity of creation, applicable to all
While your fellow human knows nothing of them at any turn
Perhaps you can be the one who listens to the greater call
And show them the intricacies of God's majestic universal laws
And help lift them from mankind's fall as a karmic cause.

If you can choose to espouse only that which is purifying
And apply the power of the mind and pranayama breathing
And feel love for the masses living with resentment seething
Then you will extend your life while they
Will continue on prematurely dying.

If you can use your will in perpetually purifying
Body, mind, emotion and this becomes your mission and you enjoy it,
While the masses live despondent live and have a fear of dying
Then you will extend your life, my friend,
And move into the New Age of life extension and deploy it.

If you can go forth with a certain cocky consciousness
And know that you create every aspect of your own reality
Including health, vitality, longevity, and a sort of immortality
While all others about you succumb in their subconsciousness
To programmed beliefs of a short life full of struggle and brutality
Them you will extend your life, my friend,
And do it within the mass consensus reality.

If you can embody these ideals for longevity that you've hereby read
While everyone around you is distracted by media-based beliefs,
If you can become all that we've written about herein and said,
Then you will create your own patterns of life extension motifs.
And you will learn that you don't have to work hard at it anymore.
And you will learn that you aren't aging like the masses anymore.
You will just be the essence of life extension – do you see?

If you can choose to challenge the mass consensus reality norm
While the common man thinks that the norm is the way things are
If you decree to not identify with the norm –
        the sickly, elderly folk forlorn –
Then you will extend your life, my friend, and
        stand out like a shining star!

The Master and the Acolyte

The Master and the Acolyte were walking on the sand.
They sorrowed for the human race aging on the land.
The old and gray were always there and seen at every hand.

They turned them left; they turned them right;
        they saw that everywhere
The aged ones were all around; immortality could not be found
        except within the pair.
An old crone would shuffle by; an aged man would wheeze and die
        and always in despair.

The Master and the Acolyte were on a grand retreat.
They walked along and came upon an old and curious street.
And few were there to hear or care – yet their wisdom was complete.

The inner science (if practiced daily) is a gift of the greatest worth.
Five hundred years had come and gone for the Master since his birth.
And that was odd because it was when humans aged upon the earth

"A class, a class," the Master said, "Is what we chiefly need."
The Acolyte, he made a sign for passersby to read.
A sign of sparing words, it read, "A Class in Immortality."

The light, it fell to left; it fell to right; it lit the sign where it was shown.
The words they seemed to scintillate as if chiseled out of stone.
A few were greatly moved by it and wanted the wisdom for their own.

Three were there to heed the pair; the sign, it would not let them pass.
The Master said, "Now take your seats, we will begin the class."
But this was odd, there were no seats, they sat upon the grass.

An older man, one of the talkative types
        got up and coughed and spoke,
"To live a thousand years…" said he,
        but here he had to have a smoke,

"Is what I chiefly seek…" but there, his voice
        was low and weak and broke.
Said another, one of the portly lot, "My mind is willing,
        but my body's not."
Said a third, "My chores, I could drop,
        but who then would tend my shop?"

"The time is now," the Master said, "to talk of immortality.
"Of death and aging and of how powerful the mind can be,
"Of ashrams and India and of immortality for you and me."

"In the Himalaya's, there are those who are nine hundred years old.
"Though of them you've never heard, nor has a word of it been told,
"If mastery of the inner science is perfected, there is no aging to unfold."
The Master taught the class, and these were the words he said.
"Immortality," said he, "cannot be found in something that you've read.
"It comes from practicing the powers of the mind and breath instead."

"It will have to do with you and the thoughts
        of immortality that you accrue,
"And if those thoughts become you,
        they can create a transformation that can undo,
"Aging, and if coupled with the fast and the breath,
        the whole body can renew."

"It is utilizing the long-fast to rid the body of
        toxins and senescence cells for rejuvenation
"It is mastering the pranayama breathing cycle
        to add great amounts of prana for regeneration."

"There are other practices and cannons
        and secret rites that are very good
"You should daily cleanse yourself of fear and hate
        and limiting beliefs, if you would
'Fasting, and bathing, and the five-element cleansing
        Are there to do, and you should."

"It is raising your vibration closer to the Creator's eternal light.
"It is rising up from baseness to espouse the love of what is right.
"It is abstaining from the impure food and drink and the addictive rum.
"It is lending a helping hand to those who are blind or deaf or dumb."
"It is transforming the gross body with the power
        of the concentrated mind,
"Connected with the power of the breath and the fast
        into a body of the lighter kind."
"Meditation and concentration are two of the things
        you will need to learn…"

And here the Master ceased his speaking,
        and the surrounding silence seemed to burn.
The Acolyte, he broke the silence saying,
        "Let us meditate and concentrate in turn."

The Acolyte, he lit a candle and said to concentrate
        upon the flickering flame.
He said to concentrate for two minutes keeping
        as still as a painted figure in a frame.
Then to close the eyes for ten minutes holding
        the flame image steady and the same.

The students all thought this too much work and a bit absurd.
When it was time he said, "Let's all come back,"
        but nothing at all was ever heard.
And that was hardly odd because…they'd all
        quietly left without saying a word!

In Pursuit of Longevity

Is potential longevity
Something you can see
And relate to tangibly?

It will have to do with you
And new beliefs that will lead to
An expectation and anticipation that you too
Can maintain your bodily form in youthfulness
With an understanding of thoughts that bless,
When you learn to accept that *'Thought Is'*
The force of creation in every human's incarnation quiz.
When you know that what you think is what you create,
When you accept that your thoughts dictate your own fate,
When you realize that if you don't expect to age,
     you won't age,
In the same way that the masses age,
     who are caught inside the cage,
Of the aging agreement that now runs rampant in the world,
In which, one to another, your health or sickness is hurled
Into the mass consciousness that measures all the same
And creates the expectation to follow along
     in the aging game.

You do not pull yourself out of it
And create new beliefs, bit by bit.
If you can do that and keep yourself as fit as you can,
And become a toxin-free woman or a man,
And spurn addictive habits that hurt and burn,
And support yourself along your planetary sojourn,
And avoid negative emotions in all that you do or say,
And utilize the power of love in each and every day.

If you can do all of this, all the time and steadfastly,
Then you will be heading for a very long life and longevity!
This constitutes the basics of longevity
And sets the stage for a long life that is free
Of premature aging and disease.
An older man or woman you can be with a youthful ease.

The Song of Methuselah

If you should ask me whence these stories,
Whence these legends and traditions,
Of man immortal, man the ageless,
Whence these stories have arisen,
I should answer; I should tell you,
From the garden known as Eden,
Come these stories; come these legends.

In the Eden, men were different,
Were much kinder, were so gentle,
Lived with love and grace and caring,
Love was everywhere among them,
Lived with peace and much compassion,
Made their neighbor's joy important,
Had no envy nor resentment,
Had respect and admiration.

In the garden known as Eden,
Lived a man they called Methuselah.
He came to be a living legend,
Lived the longest in the Eden,
Nine hundred years and sixty-nine,
Were all the years of old Methuselah.

Devils from the camp of Satan,
Did disturb the peace of Eden,
Whispered in the ears of men then,
Prompted men to selfish action,
Tempted men to break the Sabbath,
Led to conquest and great carnage.

The air it changed and led to aging,
Aging came to man the ageless,
Death was next to follow aging.
The end of Eden did come after.
Only memories now are left us,
Only legends do remain now.

In the Beginning When There Was No Aging

To L. Ashley, 2012

When man was first projected onto the earth
In Eden – he was immortal – a gift for humanity's birth.
There was no aging to mar humanity's sense of self-worth.

But, from realms much higher than that of man
There arose a magnanimous master plan
And when inaugurated, the gift of death began.

In Eden, the air was different than today.
Xenon was in the air, and it had a role to play.
It engendered regeneration in a greater way.

But the xenon in the air was removed.
The energy of regeneration became diffused.
And then men began to age, and death ensued.

Whisperings from the fallen ones were next in line.
Promptings to act in self-interest serving to incline,
Men to gradually gravitate to power, greed, and wine.

And the history of mankind from that point on,
Is recorded in the annuals of warfare thereupon,
A sad sojourn from whence the seed of man had its spawn.

But now a new turning of the heavens rolls on its way,
Man enters the Age of Aquarius and hopes of a better day,
And the promise of a new immortality that will return to stay.

Healing 101

O' how could you ever lose your health,
If you know by heart the cure for every ill,
And have on every level, the healer's skill?

O' how could you ever harbor fear of disease,
If you shun the fearful thoughts of your peers,
And revel in joy whenever creativity appears?

O' how could you not reach immortality,
If you keep the vibration of health on high,
And shun limitation in all that you see,
How could you miss the bliss of the immortal kiss?

Simple Simon and the Highman

Says Simple Simon to the Highman, "Show me health."
Says the Highman to Simple Simon, "Show me first your
       cures a'plenty.
Says Simple Simon to the Highman, "Indeed, I have not any."

Says Simple Simon to the Highman, "Show me Longevity."
Says the Highman to Simple Simon, "Show me first that you can
       live fearlessly."
Says Simple Simon to the Highman, "Alas, I fear disease will
       come to me."

Says Simple Simon to the Highman, "Show me immortality,"
Says the Highman to Simple Simon, "Show me first that you can
       regenerate at will."
Says Simple Simon to the Highman, "Alas, I must take my pill."

Popping Out of the Aging Box

What if you play the first game?
It's the same old path that you've always walked
And you'll age just as surely as the tick of a clock.

But what if you play the second game?
It's a future's game that opens the lid,
For extended life spans, it puts in a bid,
To honor your body by fasting whereby toxins are rid,
And pranayama breathing becomes your way,
And immortal thought patterns light your day,
Where you imagine you are becoming the immortal guru,
Commanding cell regeneration of a new you,
With a body, youthful and vigorous with a creative feel,
Where vibrations of love, joy, and zest appeal,
Where you utilize the great power of the universe,
Mental emanations to halt aging and reverse,
Some of the degeneration of aging within you.
To pop out of the aging box – you, the longevity guru!

On Wishing to Be Young Again

Oh, I wish I could be young again,
When the sweet song of youth was sung,
And the future was always far, far away,
And 'old' was a word I never would say.

Oh, I wish I could be twenty-five again,
When my eyes were keen and sharp back then,
And wearing glasses was never a thought,
And glasses were something that I never bought.

Oh, I wish I could have my whole life ahead,
To plan anew all of things I want to do instead,
Of having this scourge that men call age,
Where the book of life turns page by page.

Oh, I wish we had rejuvenation again,
When lives were longer by a factor of ten,
And live for centuries like those in Atlantis back then.
The tall, peaceful 'Golden Race' - the immortal men.

The Alta-Ra, they say, had rejuvenation machines,
Their Temples of Rejuvenation, were part of the means,
That allowed them to reach a thousand years of age,
Eons ago, but now only legends appear on a page.

The Basics of Longevity

Methinks I should purview the basics
       of longevity and give you a tip or two.
First of all, it will have to do with you deciding
       that you really do want a long life span.
There's no doubt about it – you must first
       fire your will to do it – it's key to the plan.
Without a strong will to do it, nothing
       is achieved or accomplished or attained.
Your will starts the flow to go beyond
       the short life in which man is now entrained.

Second, you must choose to pursue the ways
       that lead to a long and healthy life.
Divorce the days of degenerate ways –
       take fitness, healthy food and drink to wife.
Cast out smoking, drinking, drugs and the like –
       the ways of a degenerate spouse.
Bring in responsibility, creativity, sustainability
       and wellness into your house.

And lo! Let the moving finger write
       many new words to scribe another plan
For your life's purpose as you sojourn
       upon the earth whether woman or a man.
That can lead you to the land of longevity
       where now forming is a long-lived clan.
And if you follow longevity's ways, you can
       join them. Verily, yes indeed, you can!

Longevity may have a dual meaning, which
       I should now reveal to human ears.
Mankind mostly marks it with the statistical
       standard norm of a hundred years.
But some say the potential human lifespan

is between 140 and 150 years.
But to reach either goal you must strive for it,
     see it through, and as the way clears
Become your own doctor—one who can live
     without disease or illness fears.
You will eventually attract a fan club-
     and then you can bow to their adoring cheers.

You know, I must confess, I feel blessed,
     I don't worry about or fear disease – I don't.
Cancer? Veggie juicing usually keeps it at bay -
     I juice and worry about it – no I won't.
Heart disease? Exercise, raw fat and fasting
     usually corral it, and do I fear it – no, I don't.
Diabetes? Exercise, fasting, and no processed sugar
     keep it away. Do I worry – no I won't.
Dementia? Exercise and raw dairy usually prevent it.
     Me, fear it? No, I absolutely don't.
MERSA and pneumonia? Colloidal silver cures them.
     Fear them? I positively won't.

You know, I've heard it said that
     greater longevity will come about
From a greater elimination of toxins –
     certainly, a truism without doubt.
Ridding toxins from foods-thoughts-emotions –
     these are the three to the long-life route.

It would be good to bring higher knowledge
     of love into your long-life repertoire.
To follow the ways of longevity's days
     is to allow a higher self-love than ever before.
And to delve deeply into the harm
     that negative outbursts do to your body is in store.
And to fathom self-destruction caused by
     damming thoughts is going deeper than before.

Oh, I would be amiss to dismiss aging
        caused by fear and loss – I must
State that trauma from loss of job or mate
        or health affects aging, and let's trust
Studies showing that fear and trauma
        take a heavy toll in aging, and play a big role.

And so, it's good to maintain health, and enough
        wealth, and partnering as a goal,
This allows you, the longevity seeker,
        time enough to adapt and adjust.

And last, you must just relax and come to expect it.
        You must plan on knowing that you are going to live a long life.
Then you should just let it flow and know that longevity
        is your natural state if you're free of fear and strife.
Whether it's one hundred years or the full
        140 to 150, you will need to just come to expect it.
That's the key – maintain thoughts of being long lived
        and then eventually you'll discover that you'll connect to it.

Two-Line Rhyming Affirmations Couplets for Longevity

I am healthy, wealthy, wise.
I am an ageless sage who never dies.

I intend to invoke the power of my mind
To lead me over 100 years in everything I find.

I intend a long and healthy life that leads me to longevity.
I keep fit, eat healthy food and drink, and no addictions for me.

I train my mind to create thoughts of longevity every day.
I do this so consistently that it has become my way.

I rid myself of my death urge by doing things that are downright fun.
Why would I want a death urge – I put premature aging on the run.

Affirmations for Life Extension and for Benevolence Are What Create Them

Longevity's Daily Lexicon

Mornings and Maintaining

'When dawn's rosy fingers herald the newly
      dawning day, the Child-God-Man
Seeks ways of maintaining his entombing earthly
      bodily form to keep disease away
And to lengthen his sojourn upon this planetary
      plane – ways that support
His journey in the world – ways that remove
      the daily stress and strain that drain
His life force energy – ways to replenish it to nurture and sustain
      him for a longer life than before – for in the days
Of yesteryear and yore, ways to maintain his body were not
      supported – all lives were harsh and short with stern
Kings and Queens in court, but now a New Age dawns,
      and it does support
The many ways to extend the days – extend the life
      of the Child-God-Man – ways that
From a time out of mind that the human race can find –
      and some of them may even amaze!

The Western World tends to seek its answers
      in the outer workings of the Tao
By choosing fitness clubs and ritualized exercises
      that serve in the here and now.
Aerobics and resistance weights make a hearty
      workout that surely can endow
A high fitness level for maintaining robust health
      as all who embark upon it will allow.

The Eastern world tends to seek a longer stay
      through the inner workings of the Tao
And looks to meditation and the cultivation of
      the ways of gratitude to disavow
The disharmony and discord that take their daily
      deadly toll on wellness even now.

They cultivate blessings and forgiveness and
          appreciation – and all ill will they disallow.
Of the many other facets followed for maintaining
          high health on the earthly plane
Yoga, tai chi, aerobics, jogging and weight lifting
          are a few used to attain the same.
Studies show routine exercise lowers risk of –
          even cures many major diseases.
And so, longevity's lexicon will always include
          regular, repetitive exercise that seizes.
The attention of the longer life span seeker by
          an impulse that prods and pleases.

In the far East, the morning Aarti sings songs of
          adoration rhyming like a mantra.
A well-known mantra is 'Om Namah Shivya,
          Om Namah Shivya, Om Namah Shivya.'
It appreciates the gift of life, blesses our
          existence, and sanctifies our being.
In the West, singing church hymns to figures of
          the faith in fondness – all agreeing,
That life is a precious gift for the seeker's soul
          to learn the lessons needed, thus freeing
It to rise to a higher plateau not yet known but
          fathomed as a futuristic distant seeing.
Adorations to creation cleanse the emotional-mental
          bodies and as such are very healing.

Meditation and concentration and working
          with the breath are widely used
To still the mind and focus on the breath to
          realize spirit and air being fused.
Incurable diseases have been cured by mastering
          the breath – it is very healing,
And in time the spirit-air interconnectedness
          becomes a universal truth revealing,

The great spirit-mind-emotional body linking
        as a wisdom learned and appealing.

Breath mastery is – and always has been – one
        of the secret paths to immortality.
Fasting mastery is another – and those who work with
        the power of the mind to break free
From aging – various yoga sutras and the Vedic texts say
        that concentration and immortality
Can be reached and realized by the student who
        learn pranayama breath mastery.
For the breath and mind are deeply intertwined
        and when the mind can find
Its focus in the breath, students who master
        the breath eventually come to see
The seventy-two thousand energy channels or
        nadi lines where energy and
Nutrients flow throughout the physical and subtle
        bodily sheaths, and let me mention
That short of immortality, practicing pranayama breathing
        properly can lead to life extension.
Breath mastery is a major way to reach your true
        potential as any master knows – of 140 to 150 years –
And that, we agree, would be a major achievement
        and not inconsequential!

Noontimes and Nutrition

When the sun reaches zenith, lunchtime nears
        with its food cravings, but also with some food fears.
And rightly so, all of you should know that your
        foods are compromised even though
Much promotion is done to assuage food fears
        and ensure that public patronage is won.
Many problems exist within the foods that are
        stocked in your grocery stores at this time.
Cancer, heart disease, diabetes, and dementia
        are all linked to them – it is a crime!
Degenerative disease did not exist before processed foods arrived.
        but they are here, the diseases are serious –
And they are systemic, and exist worldwide.

Let us look at the problems with many major food
        groups in your grocery stores:
Foods cooked in oil create cooked fat which will deposit plaque
        in those arteries of yours.
Processed sugar in many foods and in all pastries
        contributes to diabetes – it's difficult to use and eliminate.
Can you not hear my entreaties?

Cooked meat contains a heterocyclic amine toxin
        which causes a thirty percent higher
Cancer risk and also contains antibiotics and karmic
        residues from slaughtered flesh, and this explains
The rise of antibiotic resistant MERSA
        bacteria strains, which remains.
Also know that non-organic fruits and veggies
        are grown in a pesticidal soup
Known to contribute to cancer – the truth of
        this, agribusiness tries to dupe.
They're grown without love and care by workers
        of low concern and vibration.

You'll come to praise the best foods grown with
        care and love and adoration.
It is callous that fossil fuels are squandered by
        shipping foods across the seas.
Higher consciousness prizes local foods and
        shuns foreign foods with ease.
Internet articles on, "Foods You Should Avoid" –
        read and head this advice.
Helping hands are out there for the human race – it's
        accurate – you shouldn't need to think twice.
Pollution runs rampant. You should buy filtered
        water and organic produce.
Read the labels – many foods you thought
        fine, you should avoid or reduce.
Let us speak now about some healthy food tips
        that may take you back.
Eating oranges with avocados constitutes,
        or is nature's aphrodisiac.
Raw eggs slightly help your heart, but cooked eggs
        can slightly harm your heart.

Many say that the Mediterranean diet is a better choice,
        but the Vonderplantiz Primal Diet can play a part
In reaching 140 to 150 years – it is unpasteurized dairy,
        raw veggie juice, fruits, eggs, unsalted nuts, seeds, unheated
honey, cooked starches and legumes. These go
        far into supplying vitamin and mineral needs and reducing
the toxic load from food, drink, and air – and so,
        the longevity seeker should select foods and drink with care.
        Eggs were given to man as nature's most nearly perfect food.
They contain protein and raw fat that detoxifies,
        and when eaten raw they are a good food for the truly wise.
It is important to know that raw fat is a very important nutrient,
        because it detoxifies the body, and the joints it lubricates.
Raw dairy is unpasteurized raw milk and it is hard to get in
        many USA states, and it consists of raw milk, cream,

butter and cheese, and you can get raw milk from cow
        share programs in most USA states, and if you can get it,
it would be wise to add it to your dinner plates.

The raw food Vonderplantiz Primal Diet is the diet for
        longevity and life extension, but it includes raw meat and
in this there are some things I wish to mention.

Any meat, cooked or raw, always involves the slaying of an
        animal, and so, any cooked meat that humans eat – to the
belly full will always contain a toxin called
        heterocyclic amine that ups the cancer risk by thirty
percent, and also some say the animal's fear on being
        slain – apart from its torment will download into the
meat-eaters body and in time will weaken it, and so, as the
        seeker matures, he or she may eventually have to
admit that there are some problems with eating meat and
        then they may choose to give up on it.

Unheated honey is another power food in the Primal Diet
        that acts like insulin.
It helps nutrients get through cell walls so that more
        nutrients can get within, but the key word here is unheated –
all supermarket honeys have been heated,
        which reduces them to sugar and then any enzyme value
is thus defeated.

Fresh veggie juicing will supply three times your body's
        daily vitamin-mineral needs, and then your body's regen-
eration thereby proceeds.

And last starch-based foods and legumes are best
        assimilated when cooked –
They are the Primal Diet's raw food exception and should
        not be overlooked.
Unroasted, unsalted nuts and seeds and unheated oils
        round out the Primal Diet that experts say we are pro-
grammed for, and it equals a raw food commissariat.

Pineapple with coconut and a 1-hour hot water
        soak constitutes the lymph flush.
The heat, the coconut oil, and the pineapple's vitamin C
        make a mixture lush for internal cleansing –
which creates a deep healing rush.

There is a new product out, that I should say a word or two
        about – it is Lite Water, in which that one drop of heavy
water per gallon in all waters of the world has been
        removed.

That one drop per gallon may not seem like much, but
        it retards regeneration – in this there can be no doubt as
Hunza centenarians drink glacial melt water
        (that contains less heavy water)
and their longevity is thus improved.

And now, let us talk about the vast world of fasting,
        in which one drinks water, but eats no solid food at all for
durations that may seem everlasting, and for Eastern
        Masters, this is their immortality wherewithal.

In the western world no food seems far too contrasting –
        however, there are scientific studies showing that fasting
creates healing, but this is small compared to it its
        anti-aging effects dealing with the removal of half dead
senescent cells, and the recent research results
        revealing, that if left in place they create a
crescendo-like aging affect by secreting toxins rampaging.

Fasting can remove them, for if one drinks water and a wee
        bit of juice, but eats no solid food at all, it sets the staging
for the body to scavenge upon itself, and thus,
        absorb many of those senescent cells,
thereby freeing the body from this sort of aging –
        which then allows longevity to find its parallels.

Many fasts exist – fasting 1-day a week helps
          your digestion and it is my first suggestion.
A fast of 1-3 weeks cures disease, a fast of 1-2 months rejuvenates,
          now do you, the reader, have a question?
There are juice fasts, water-fasts, air-fasts,
          and many other types in-between.
The serious longevity seeker should add fasting -
          it will keep them lean.
And I do not hesitate to restate – it reduces the risk
          of all disease – ah yes fasting.
And after one masters it (gets used to it), fasting
          may co-create a life everlasting!

Evenings and Eros

Ah, yes, when the sun's last rosy rays slowly
        fade away, then comes the night.
And pensive people ponder on,
        'The dance of the night that brings you delight.'
Sexuality – it is the reason 80 percent of
        incarnating souls desire physicality.
But fraught with issues – legal, moral, judgmental
        is this thing called carnality.
May I remind mankind that – men and women were designed
        to deliciously fit together
In the sexual embrace that forever recalls the ecstasy
        that once made life a delight
That people do not have now, except when they play
        in the dance of the night.

In the East, it's even seen as a duty to prolong the moment
        of the clouds and the rain, for they say
that it's the closest one can come to the Infinite Creator of the All,
        and yet others choose to abstain and refrain from sex at all.

Many facts and facets and fantasies are found
        within sexuality that I would now like to expound and
expand upon and one is the heightened health that gains ground,
        for when sexuality is expressed day after day –
in a regular way – it will be found that the orgasmic experience
        is not only plainly pleasurable, it's also very healing.
It resets the energy field in a blissful blend –
        daily rancor comes to an end, and one is reeling in ecstasy.
Negative feelings and frustrations – they're gone!
        One is happy, and joyful, and playful with a zest
For life that's strong like singing a song!
        I should also say, that when sexuality is expressed

in a regular way, it keeps you younger and gray hair and
        wrinkles come to the ones who don't express it – makes
you wonder – sexuality stimulates hormonal secretions –
        the hormones of youth – it throws asunder
the normal aging toxins to some degree –
        such that a sort of youthfulness is assisted
without the need for hunger.

But many have been hurt or burned or spurned,
        and then they tend to shy away
From partnering and renounce the pleasure
        of the joining together in sexual play.
And indeed, for some if this runs its full course
        martyrdom may become the result,
Whereupon a part of life's purpose is lost
        and if this happens a therapist is needed,
For this should be addressed and healed
        because if one abstains long enough
The personality becomes warped, ill-tempered,
        irritable, negative and gruff.
Hence these traits should be analyzed and heeded.

Relationships in the ideal should express
        a real caring and sharing and daring.
You should care for your partner, dare to be
        vulnerable, and allow the airing
Of conflicts and criticisms – communication,
        communication, communication
Is key to conflict resolution in order to keep it
        a satisfying, gratifying creation.
Care for your partner in a way that is nurturing,
        stimulating and sustaining.
Dare to be vulnerable – reveal your secrets –
        leave not much remaining.
Share life's interests, joy in your jaunts,
        Discover the mutually pertaining.

There are three aspects to each and every man and woman
        that need expression.
Let us review the physical-mental-emotional triangle
        of being in short succession.
The physical – not just sex – but the hug, the holding
        of hands, the touch, the smile and such.
The mental – the thoughts, and the things
        your partner does you like so much.
The emotional – the feelings, the infatuation, the
        adoration, the fondness and such.
If one or more is missing, a lopsidedness is your
        Partnering is sure to occur
To downgrade it into a lower level of
        satisfaction you will not prefer.
Did you know that your partnerships are always better
        (with the love letter) at the start?
At first, you only see your partner's good side
        (and hope you'll never part).
But, later on (due to feelings of lack), you're taken
        aback and then focus upon only the worst.
If this downward trend continues, it may move
        into nasty words with a yelling curse.
The trick is to train your brain to make little
        of everything you don't prefer,
And meld your mind to focus on what you find that
        you do like – and this I can indeed assure –
Will surely keep things going smoothly for you
        and he or she or him or her.

Did you ever wonder if there is a spiritual reason
        that exists beneath your sexuality?
There is a reason – and ideally, it is for freely forming
        the bonded pair.
Promiscuity and casual sex are damaging.
        They impair your personality.

It is best to really care for the one you share your sexuality with.
        You should get familiar with your partner's
Thoughts and moods and motions,
        through repeated acts of intercourse
By learning their likes and dislikes and emotions.

Also, people tend to talk about sex with anyone
        except the one they share it with.
Ask your lover how you can better pleasure them
        and become your partner's love-smith.
Telepathy comes to the ones who share sex
        in a bonded pairing partnership, for when they play
In the sexual way their neurons fire and rewire
        their brains with a telepathic script.

And if you bloom in your sexuality and allow
        your sexual sensations to fully blossom,
Kundalini energy can be released to vastly
        improve your body – totally awesome!
These advanced techniques are around and if found
        can cocreate a sort of rejuvenation.
And there are other methods that exist to assist
        you to astral travel and leave your home station.
And alas, if you have no partner (although it sounds crass)
        you still have your hands,
And you can still enjoy sexual pleasure with
        masturbation – as it's called in many lands.

Have you ever wondered why your sex drive
        is so alive and blatantly strong?
It has to do with your root chakra – and it's amiss
        to dismiss this energy wheel along
The base of your spine, for it's a cone that's known
        to absorb the Earth's own energy,
Thereby increasing its energy flow far more
        than any other chakra can.

Need I mention that this creates tension which needs to be
       released in every woman and every man.
The root chakra's so strong that it lends along
       energy to other chakras when needed.
The heart (higher love) and throat (greater speech)
       often need help and are heeded.

There are lessons that burn that need to be
       learned hidden within sexuality.
Man must learn to separate his animal emotional self
       from his higher rational mentality.
Many mis-mating's have come for some who've let passion
       override common sense reality.
What is the greatest gift of all in physicality?
       It may well be the gift of your body, you see,
And this may be so, because, oh, it gives you the
       opportunity to express your sexuality
So that you can have a glimpse of what ecstasy is –
       the dance of the night that brings you delight!
Remember, it's your birthright to allow, rejoice
       and delight in the dance of the night!

Chapter 2, Poems on Life Extension

A Life Extension Love Sonnet

Ah, how sweet I heard a voice within a dream say,
"Love, is truly at the heart of all you seek.
"It is far more important to you than it may seem
"For health and youth and happiness."
This I heard it speak.

Your bodily form has sub forms – some say there are nine.
One is the Astral and it is the seat of your emotions in every way.
Your human form reflects your emotional states –
        aging or youthfulness intertwine.
People stay young and youthful or they age if
        It is Love or Hate that rules the day.

Your Astral body is the sheath you wear
        when e'er you're dreaming.
It is a replica of your body in every organ, bone and cell.
        But it's made of the finer stuff of electro-plasma streaming,
And it will deform as if in Hell, if it's Hate
        that is the State wherein you dwell.
And damage to the Astral will imprint upon
        the physical within a span of time.
But, if Love displaces Hate, healing can return
        you back into your prime.
To Love yourself and to Love all others
        is to be the Universal Brother.
And to allow a Love of Life to flourish
        in every way it can is the Healing Mother.

Isles of Life Extension

Roundabout the world oppressed
The people come and go enmeshed
In struggle, strife, forever stressed.

They've never heard of Babaji
Who sat beneath a banyan tree
And spoke of immortality.

Advanced messengers from the teaming stars
That populate this gigantic galaxy of ours
See us entombed within prison bars.

"We do live many hundreds of your years.
"We are not beset by your difficulties or your fears.
"We are emissaries and come to you as pioneers."

"Brotherhood and peace and love and joy must exist within.
"We live a blissful life that is beyond your ken to comprehend.
"Discord is your way of life, and distrust is that of your kin."

"If you could live two hundred years,
          paradoxically they say,
"It would not serve most of you – you're much too
          entangled in the fray.
"Life is too difficult for most of you – eventually you'd want
          death to come and take you away."

And yet, isles of a immortality of sorts have always been
And live in those few who choose to deeply look within.
Emil, an immortal from the Far East, spoke on how to begin.

"Youth is God's seed of love planted in the human form divine.
"Nightly, let your inner child merge into the perfected design.
"Daily ask your inner alchemist to conjure up youthfulness supine."
"Practice intense concentration and dissolve into the infinitude.

"Merge into God's brilliant light, cast out all dark energy accrued,
"Recrystallize into a state of high perfection totally renewed."

And now the spinning earth moves into
        a New Age of technological advance,
And new breakthroughs in science make
        aging a reversible happenstance.
Stem cells, new blood, removing old blood are a few
        ways to rejuvenate and enhance.

Many other treatments and many other methods
        will eventually come to the fore.
Hormone replacements, genetic interventions, magnetic
        repolarizations – these and many more science will ex-
plore and then a whole new rejuvenation will land on the
        many isles of immortality and humans will once again
rejuvenate as they did in Atlantis many eons before.

Ode to Life Extension

Physical immortality -
Can it be?
Or has it been lost in antiquity?

O' there have been tales told
        of immortals both new and old.
In antiquity, there was a man named Methuselah who lived
        nine hundred sixty-nine years as we are told.
And in ancient Atlantis there are accounts that we can read
        of a majestic machine that used magnetic re-polarization
To seed the reversal of aging. This Temple of Rejuvenation of old
        is now gone but its legend lingers and holds fascination.

In the Age of Atlantis, there was said to be a group of humans
        who were the first life extension pioneers.
These peaceful people, called the Alta-Ra, were said
        to live a thousand years.
They used advanced healing, cultivated concentration
        and developed a technological device called
The Temple of Rejuvenation, and all of this enabled them to reach
        astonishing lifespans and it surely does entice.

And we can read of the Taoist in China
        and meet immortals there.
Although the Chinese idolize their eight immortals
        most are unaware
That there are immortals now who live in Taoist communities
        in near seclusion and do not shout it out.
At eleven years, as part of his training, a Taoist acolyte
        was taken to meet one of them
The Bat Immortal was tall, thin, smooth skin, and had eyes
        that were shining like a gem.
"He cultivates the great Yin and avoids the light,"
        the acolyte was told.

"He has memorized all the Taoist Cannons,
          and he eats his food cold."

And there were other immortals that the acolyte
          over a period of time got to see.
They took animal totem names, they all were adepts, and all
          used different ways to attain their immortality.
The Yin-Yang Immortals explored the ever shifting
          Tao in different ways.
Yin in meditation, Yang in outer exploration of the
          Tao inner-outer maze.
Master Sun, the immortal, had seen many
          Chinese dynasties come and go.
The Frog Immortal filled with chi gave
          the acolyte a levitation show.

Or we can read in modern times the tale of a
          British Colonel who had found
A lamasery in the Far East where aged lamas
          had a youthfulness to astound.
This aged colonel had gray hair, a stooped back,
          and walked with a cane.
But he stayed with them and adapted to their ways and
          after two years he was a younger man once again.

O' these are the tales of the immortals in
          ages both old and new.
But can you conceive of the austerity that they
          musts practice and do?
Could you renounce the world and eschew
          all of its social scenes?
Could you keep away from mainstream life
          and end all that it means?
Could you daily sequester yourself in a
          mental meditative repose,

In order to become the immortal master
        that you and I suppose?
Could you practice concentration until
        your face turns the color blue?
Could you master the manipulation
        of form so that it pleases you?
Could you do all of these things and still
        keep your life almost the same?
What price would you pay to become
        master of the immortality game?
O' alchemy in the Age of Aquarius
        will blossom forth and unfold.
Long life will come to the future human
        without the austerity of old.
The path to the immortality of the past
        will not meld in the new mold.

But the wiser way will be a mixed blending
        of the old with the new.
A higher plateau of the evolution of the soul
        is part of the path to pursue.
And the use of life extension affirmations that make use
        of the new longevity revelations to accrue
A higher use of the mind in its ability to create
        predominant thought patterns of you
Becoming one who will extend their life through
        the power of the mind and the breath and the fast
With a purpose to infuse new thought patterns and
        energy and toxins into and out of you.

And this will be coupled with a proliferation of new external
        tools that will be created and developed with a purpose to
heal and imbue the aged ones with a healed
        and rejuvenated bodily form that will be totally healed and
remade anew.

O' all of these things will all lead to a far longer life span
        for the human population as historians eventually will find
and indeed, life extension, or a sort of physical
        immortality, is predicted to become the reality
seven generations after 2012, especially if benevolence
        becomes the way of humankind.

Perfection Is Immortality – Immortality is Perfection

It's what you need to learn and it's all you need to learn

Perfection means one who has overcome
        all limitation and attained immortality.
Words easy to say, but quite hard to attain, and
        they imply a high spirituality.
Perfection is purification of man's bodily sheaths
        into advanced states of vitality.
Purification of the three body sheaths: the physical body,
        the astral body and it's link to emotionally,
and the aetheric body and it's link to mentality.

Perfection implies that the physical body and
        its consciousness has been thoroughly purged
of all illness and disease – and especially the death
        urge. It means that in perfection, one attains
a consciousness where illness cannot begin.
        It means that in perfection, the death urge is curbed
and all thoughts of it do repulse.

Perfection is in he who is cleansed and purified
        of all illness and disease.
It may surprise you to learn that illness and disease
        are maladies of ill at ease
within the mentality and emotionality that mankind
        entertains and sees – if he or she can choose
a greater love for the self and all others
        he or she can be free of most of these.

Perfection requires a powerful healing to become
        an accomplished fact to negate,
the non-harmonious state – healing is purifying
        the body from a diseased fate,

and it requires a complimentary healing of the
        inner consciousness to relate to wholeness –
a reflection of the perfected state of heath that we
        contemplate.

Perfection requires a powerful healing of the death urge
        to allow a continuation of the life journey –
easiest to do if the journey has been mostly pleasant.
        But if the journey has been mostly struggle –
then one longs for a cessation.

To reach perfection is to transform the journey into a
        joyous harmonious present.

Purifying the consciousness is freeing it from being
        enmeshed in the death urge,
so deeply ingrained that the human expectation
        is for life and death to merge,
so deeply seated that it may take four life times
        to totally eradicate this scourge,
but don't be discouraged from starting now to rid yourself
        of this in an ongoing continuous purge.

Perfection has many facets and faces and
        purification practice that are used.
Mastery of the mind in which the powers of the mind
        are perfected but are never misused.
The power of thought to create is extensively explored, and
        if a Master is able to fuse his body as a youthful
thought-form into his aetheric sheath and recreate a
        youthful body, then Master is bemused.

Perfection has many facets and faces and
        purification practice that are used.
A Master is one who is able to live in an almost
        continuous state of joy without consternation.

A Master creates his or her day of bliss at the start
        of every day by the saying of an affirmation
that goes something like this: "Today is a good day. I have
        the consciousness to create it that way because I can
solve, resolve, or deal with any situation, issue or
        problem that comes up in such a way that the
outcome will always be benevolent for me." Masters
        transform these issues into Most-Benevolent-Outcomes
for a nearly constant state of joy every day,
        do you see?

Perfection has many facets and faces and purification
        practices that are used.
Breath purification is a major practice in which various
        breath cycles are studied, learned and used.
A master knows that the physical body is an energy system
        and if more energy can be added then good health
is earned – longevity returned – and this is true when the
        lungs, throat and nostrils work as a synergistic team
for then the body will have more energy it can use for the
        regeneration and repair of tissues of all sorts simply by the
mastery of breathing air.

Life extension utilizes many types of breathing practices
        and herein are two from the mix.
In pranayama breath work there is a hold at the end
        of each exhale and inhale in a timed count.
One count might be: exhale to a count of six, hold to a
        count of six, inhale to a count of four, and hold to a count
of six and this is continued for eighty rounds or so or
        until there is a blend of benefits - the rounds and
holds can vary in amount.

In connected breathing there is no hold - the exhale
        immediately follows the inhale
in a faster than normal breathing rhythm and this brings in
        vast amounts of air and some accounts detail

that after an hour of this, it often brings up a deep-seated
          trauma and it never seems to fail that the breather weeps
as the trauma come up and afterwards the
          breather no longer has to bear.
Trainees in connected breathing may connect the inhale-
          exhale in a twenty-breath cycle rhythm to complete a
breath work session – twenty cycles being the key.

Masters call the in-breath 'The Activity of Spirit' and the
          out-breath, is 'The Movement of Air'.
Masters in pranayama breathing may do longer pranayama
          breath work sessions to accrue a clear mind and
a physical vehicle that is infused with chi energy that they
          can use to maintain an oxygenated, healthy and youth-
ful body.

Perfection has many facets and faces and purification
          practices that are used.
Fasting mastery is a major practice used to remove
          senescent cells and deeply buried toxins.
Masters do periodic long-fasts of one to two months and
          during their long-fasts, all foods are refused.
Only water is consumed, but herbal tea or a little juice is
          allowed and is one of the options.
There is a story of a 76-year-old man who underwent a
          48-day fast and his results certainty were heaven sent,
because his amazed doctors said it gave him ten
          more years of life.
Ah yes, the long-fast – it rids toxins, adds years to
          your life, and removes many dietary sins.

There are many purification practices and here are a few.
Here are some of purification practices that the masters do.
Mastery of the breath for purification – air and spirit merge.
Mastery of the long-fast removes toxins, the aging scourge.
Mastery over wanting an ending – purging the death urge.
Mastery over food and drink – consuming only the pure.

Mastery over emotions – compassion the greatest for sure.
Mastery over thoughts – what's best for all – in a mirror.
Mastery over sleeping – learning you can stay awake.
Mastery over gratification – learned for mastery's sake.
Mastery of kindness – never use words that could berate.
Mastery of forgiveness – forgiving easily in any conflict.
Mastery of gratitude – being grateful for good in all of it.
Mastery of joy – creating benevolence – nothing is strict.

There is the tale of Sri Aurobindo and the Mother on
        perfection and he felt it could be attained in his fifth stage
of his ladder of ascending consciousness, and in
        that direction of perfection he wisely went and it did
slow to some degree the rate at which he aged, while
        his spiritual partner – the Mother – made attaining physical
immortality her life's mission, and she filled her
        physical vessel with spiritual light so diligently that
although her goal wasn't reached it increased her vitality
        so much so that her inner light could be seen and felt as a
sort of glow at night.

There are many guidelines for beginning your own personal
        perfection and the first step is to start to reprogram your-
self as a life extender.

Every morning affirm, "My thoughts recreate me as a life
        extension reflection," and if you can do this daily, you will
literally become a reality bender.

Next add another affirmation, "My day is steeped in
        benevolence. I affirm that only good things will happen,
and they do – they become my prevalence."

Make some changes – minor or major – in your nutritional
        food and drink intake.
Reduce convenience foods, cooked fats, pastries, sugars –
        all of these you can forsake.

Better is the Mediterranean Diet and best is the Primal Diet
        and these are diets that a life extender may choose
to partake.

Begin to add daily breath work sessions – Pranayama,
        Connected and other breathing rhythms – read up on it –
add exhalation-inhalation cycles in a sort rhythmic
        weaving.

Add weekly fasting, play with the different fasting durations,
        and before leaving this topic, know that it has always been
a major practice of the ancient immortals and they
        learned to master the long-fast inside their sacred
sanctuary walls, and they also purify their consciousness
        such that no disease or illness ever befalls.

Masters also know how to handle light in their relaxed
        meditative states, and they visualize light streaming in
through their crown's interdimensional gates, where it
        lights up and adds more energy to their aertheric
body at faster rates.

And so, these are a few guidelines you can follow and do
        for your own connection to your own perfection.
To purify your consciousness into perfect freedom from all
        illness or disease is hard to fully fathom.
Humanity and humanity alone creates all that humans
        suffer from – and this is learned in slow degrees.
Purification involves purging discord from every organ,
        tissue, cell, and even every atom.
Perfecting the body is an art that requires great dedication
        and intention and doing the work of perfection invites the
perfected state and let me mention that the innate
        capacity to heal and have a rejuvenation
intervention is not yet awakened but it will be when higher
        consciousness gets more attention.

Now in nourishment intake for longevity's sake here again
          are some changes you should make.
Avoid addictions, eat mostly raw foods except for starches
          and legumes and embrace the life extensions diets – raw
vegetables, fruits, raw eggs, unpasteurized dairy,
          unheated oils, unroasted, unsalted nuts and seeds,
unheated honey, but cooked starches and legumes –
          nutrients that can assist your life extension remake.

Masters know that thought forms the basis of creation in all
          created spheres and in the sphere of health, thoughts of ill
health create it – thus reducing one to tears
          and in the sphere of life extension, status quo
thoughts of current lifespans create a short life full of fears.
          Adoration mantras sung to the Creator purify thoughts and
then perfection nears.

Mastery over human misery is what the Buddha came here
          to do and the Buddha said to accept things the way they
are and do not rue what you cannot change, accept
          'What Is' and know that 'What Is' is right for the
civilization's current queue, and then learn serenity, and
          gratefulness and grace – so that you can to receive an
emotional breakthrough.

The mission of Master Jesus was to sway the emotional
          side of the human race away from its existing harsh, cruel
rivalry by using sermons to help displace It more
          towards a kinder, gentler people that could act and
speak with love in place and for two hundred years after
          his mission took place the world was indeed somewhat
less harsh and sometimes less base.

The Masters practice forgiveness and in any conflict, they
          truly seek a peace and this is done in several steps with
care, preparation, and apologies to release the ill will –

first, in meditation forgiveness is sought, and accepted so
that the anger can cease – and second, in
        person, a gift is given and forgiveness is asked for allow-
ing the Master's life extension to increase.

When you start your purification practices you should fast
        one day a week and then periodically, you should fast lon-
ger when you have mastered this technique – that
        is what the masters do and this will help to seal the purifi-
cation that you seek.

Then slowly assimilate the other purification practices of
        which we have talked about and herein speak, and know
that of purification and perfection, you the reader,
        have indeed been given a peek.

Negative Thoughts and Emotions Cause Afflictions

Can you not see that your thoughts and emotions
       create what is to be?
Thought is at the heart of what creates – it is the
       primary force.
If you feel unhappy or resentful or worried – feelings
       that we
humans habitually harbor, they trigger thoughts
       that divorce –
happiness and cause the preponderant course
       of our mind,
to engage in thinking chronic images of the more
       negative kind –
and they are things that create what will unfortunately,
       in due time
download their manifestation into the body's organs
       and will form
a dysfunctional condition, and then after that,
       a new illness is born.

If say, there is one who cannot see their way out of a
       difficult situation
And if they harbor long term thoughts of resentment
       and agitation,
then these thought patterns may eventually manifest
       into a cataract
to mirror the underlying thoughts in tissue –
       clouding the eyes as a fact!

Or, on another tract, women are born with a need
       to nurture – but some will suppress it
and their breasts may grow a tumor to reflect the
       needed growth and symbolically express it.

Or consider the case of a man who loses his job that
        supported and sustained him.
Bone cancer may result – the growth in cells mimicking
        the lost job's support that maintained him.

And if one maintains persistent thought patterns that
        life offers them not much
and indulges in constant bickering and bitterness –
        all negative and venomous as such,
and if the affliction called dementia eventually emerges
        from out of all of this,
why should it surprise? The symbol of the misused mind
        is very hard to miss.

Consider now those who are drawn to attain power and
        monetary goals.
Some adopt addictive habits to temper tensions that
        torture such souls,
And if this friction should cause a heart condition,
        why should it surprise?
The heart is love and a diseased heart is a message
        not too hard to surmise.

Now, let us look at what can be said for one who has
        become a diabetic.
The gland responsible for processing sweet foodstuffs
        is a sympathetic
symbol directly reflecting whether the life in progress is
        sweet or sour.
And a failed pancreas reflects a lack of sweetness –
        a message rather dour.

Time after time we are faced with this one overwhelming
        conclusion –
That men and women alone are the cause of all of the
        ills that afflict them.

And the symbols that reside inside of their tribulations
        in profusion
Gives clues and queues on how to solve and resolve and
        cure them.
Can you not see that the thought patterns you harbor
        habitually can be –
The culprits and the cur of the health problems that you
        do not prefer?
Your thoughts affect every aspect of your life including
        your health and wellbeing.
If your personality contains a negative trait, it will create
        a negative thing,
and if the focus of its creation is a negative health issue –
        in time it will manifest and sting!

To avoid creating health conditions, your thoughts
        and emotions must image yourself as well.
Your imagination to create thought images –
        is as I can surely tell
one of your greatest gifts, but most men and women
        misuse it – it's used it in a way
that creates illness and malady and struggle, and so,
        your challenge in every day
is to create preponderant thoughts that you are healthy
        and that your health is here to stay.

Can you not see that your thoughts and emotions form
        the basis of what will be?
And when your preponderant thoughts and emotions
        are on some discordant issues –
why would it surprise you that this might download into
        your very own tissues?

Shelves and Boxes

In 2008, box and shelve and drawer and rack
Were built to hold the many tools and parts and bric-a-brac
Needed to support the building of devices as it went.
For rejuvenation, the inspiration always heaven sent.
An hombre named Lopez helped for a little while and then was gone.
He helped build bench and box and drawer and then moved on.
Three years ago, he said, diabetes had come to him
"God must hate me," says he with a hateful grin.
"Not at all," says I," It is a reflection that the universe gives to you.
"Diabetics cannot absorb sugar or sweetness in food or drink.
"Your condition says your life lacks sweetness – sad but true.
"Your disease is a symbol that points to the cure – as if words in ink."

Reaching for Life Extension

Can life extension
Capture your attention
And turn you towards your inner dimension?

Some will want to go beyond
the path of simply living long
and mere longevity will only correspond
to not long enough for they are strong.
Not in muscle, but in the power to prolong
their lives through a shear 'Will-To-Do'
leading them to life spans of over six score.
Becoming way showers for extending life up to
one hundred twenty years and even more!

An important goal is to seek perfection of the soul.
Life lessons of the soul reflect separation from the whole. Twelve
Universal Laws were given to mankind that
might be imagined as a scintillating scroll,
and the Law of Karma has caused discord with
        a very heavy toll.
And the Law of Love will assist man in his evolutionary
        role of casting the ball of 'Life Extension,'
and causing it to roll.

A life extender can speak to his body's vast assemblage
        of millions of specialized cells
with words compelling and full of a general's command
        that override his culture's discombobulating yells.
Words that can trigger cell regeneration upon demand.

A life extender can tell a dividing cell where to find
        the key
whereby a new stem cell can replace an aged cell
        to some degree.

The key is in interdimensional stem cell DNA
        where time
has no meaning or relevance at all allowing life
        extension to break free.

A life extender knows how use the spoken word as
        a mental broom
to speak and sweep aging away and steadfastly stay
        in a youthful bloom.
He or she keeps his or her health and knows how to heal,
        and lives life with a playfulness.
He or she keeps fit and stays flexible and lives life with a
        purpose and a zestfulness.

Meditation and concentration and cultivation and yogic
        breathing and the long-fast make a set
of tools for radical life extension used by the Masters
        of Tibet.
Meditation of the mind and stillness of the body and
        entertaining
thoughts of immortality which are intermingled with
        maintaining
concentration on a breathing rhythm whereupon
        each and every breath flows in and out in a
timed pattern precisely preset – these form the basis
        whereby a master can change age
into youth even yet.

And added to this, a master can cultivate so much energy
        that eventually his or her eyes can illume
and shine like a rosette.

Indeed, this poem's expression of life extension sessions
        forms such an intensive progression that even
I cannot forget!

A Television Special – Living to One Hundred Fifty

Indeed, in the year 2008, a television special was aired, on,
"Living to One Hundred Fifty," – many million eyes
      watched and stared.
"Could this really be real?" many million voices seemed
      to say or said.
But most kept to their disbelief and their fear of death
      and their dread.
Yet slowly it did begin to open up the door for humans to
      begin living one hundred fifty years and more.
And by the year 2022, time had marched on, and 14 years
      had come and gone since then.
And now, new revelations have been given to humanity on
      how long the human body is designed to live.
New revelations say that your body is designed for more
      than 300 years – and even more it can give.
And futurist have received glimpses of how long men
      and woman will live and when.
Futurist say that in 10 to 20 generations people will
      be living 200 years and in a much more evolved
world by then. Your body design is for stem cells to
      replace old cells – and this you can help to happen by lib-
erating yourself from being confrontational and
      combative – amen!
Eventually humans may learn how to manipulate matter –
      or the remaking of the atoms - and then lifespans will really
soar – increasing by factors of nine or ten.

Tidal Pools and Living to One Hundred Fifty

To D. Fisler

Oh, it will be easier to live 150 and more
If you can work with this little metaphor
Of a vast sea and its surrounding seashore
Of tidal pools that form when the tide goes out,
And those countless little tidal pools can no doubt
Form and flaunt and flout and forget about
The sea since for them it has ceased to be
Because they are isolated and free
From the clinging waters of the sea.

And they can be symbols for you and me
To show us symbolically that we too can be free
From and disconnected from the clinging sea
Of humanity – and in this we can break free
From the fate of early aging and decrepitude
Which is surely the state of the sea of men and woman -
By utilizing this idea of isolation with no need to be rude -
We can be free from the sea of premature aging – yes, we can!

Oh yes, you can –
Flaunt those degenerative traits
Open wide life extension's gates
You and your long-lived associates.

Oh yes, it will be
Easier to live to one hundred fifty and more
When life extension's systems you start to explore.
Those techniques of the Taoist – those Chinese
Some living hundreds of years without having disease,
Or techniques from India as taught by Master Babiji –
Spiritual purification and spiritual community.

Oh, it will be easier
To live to one hundred fifty if you apply
The teachings of the immortality schools by and by
And if the creeds of life extension's golden rule you satisfy.
Then you can go on and on and on and not die
Regardless of he or she who may question how or why –
Purification is the one all-pervasive key.
Purify the body, the mind, and the emotions – those three
Are the steps to an extended lifespan and even immortality!
And, oh yes, you can still open wide life extension's door
If you utilize the new discoveries of science to underscore
Enhanced regeneration and healing for many, many years more.

A Challenge on Living to 150

Oh, you want to live a long life, but why?
Perhaps you're just afraid to die.
I challenge you – "Why live so long?"
"What is the reason in poetry or song"?

"I just do," you say.
"That's no reason," I rebut.
"But I really do," you say.
"For what reason," I ask, "What?"

The love of life is the reason to want more life.
What is the point of prolonging pain and strife?
To push beyond what has ever been before.
To be a way shower on opening up the immortal door.

To pursue the wondrous art of living the love of life.
To espouse the delightful joy as in the flowering of a new wife.
If you can fully fathom this your love of life will be stronger.
Your 'love of life' is the main reason to want to live longer!

The Basics of Life Extension

Now to go beyond longevity into life extension,
    here's what you'll need to do.
You'll need to remove old half dead cells, limiting beliefs,
    and negative emotions to name a few,
And become aware of how damaging and aging
    these things are to your bodily form and you.
Masters remove old half dead cells by fasting a month
    or more – it's tried and true.
Next, add new cells, new unlimited beliefs, and
    new beloved emotions to undo
The signs and symptoms and rampaging of aging –
    a sorry song, but oh so sad and true.

For new cells – intension, pranayama breathing,
    fasting and the raw food Primal Diet.
For limiting beliefs – immortality school affirmations to undo
    limiting beliefs with life extension affirmations to seed the clue.
For higher consciousness use gratitude, forgiveness and kindness
    to let loving thoughts come to you.
For fasting, the serious student should give it
    a fair chance and not disaster it.
For breath work, the serious student should learn
    pranayama breathing and master it.
For a better diet, the serious student should try
    a diet like the raw food Primal Diet and adopt it.
For meditation, go into no-space, no-time (the great void)
    and become very quiet and very still.

Meditation is one of your greatest healing tools
    because it gets you past your drama.
It allows you to just be – to just exist – and in that state –
    freed from negative emotions
Your body will return to its natural balance and health
    With a feeling of wellbeing like the calmest oceans

And in meditation you can also release and heal old traumas.

The life extender should take better and better care
        of their physical body and
Treat their body as the most precious thing that
        they own, you see –
Because it is – it is what allows you to be here –
        so, keep it as healthy as it can be.
Beyond this, you should also know that your body
        has an amazing ability to heal.
And then you will need to just come to expect it
        the way a child expects each day to be fun and good.
When you can do these things then it will come as it
        should because you are the one who directs it.
And in time you might get a glimpse of the human drama
        that depicts us – that we humans alone
Are the creators of all of ills that afflict us.

Life Extension's Modus Operandi

The 1ˢᵗ Level Beginning Daily Practices

Remember, your body Is designed to live
        well over 200 years
and when you do the daily practices an
        extended life span appears.

<u>The Affirmations</u>

Affirmations are at the heart of becoming a
        life extender.
They form the basic tools needed to become
        a reality bender.
They can bend your reality and literally re-script it
        with new pair of glasses.
And indeed, your physical reality as a life extender
        can go far beyond the masses
just by simply re-conditioning your mentality.

Daily, every morning as soon as you get out of bed
        and your feet hit the floor,
something like the following affirmation should be said:

"I affirm that I am a life extender and I am going
        to extend my life and that is all there is to it!"
"I am a life extender and I am a reality bender –
        I do the practices and I know I will do it!"

Affirmations are also at the heart of working towards
        becoming a future human.
Two hundred years beyond 2012, in the future human's
        day, every day may well begin
with an affirmation paraphrased in a very practical way
        so as to create a good day.
Ten generations past 2012, futurists see a world far
        more benevolent than it is now.

Every morning you should say an affirmation like this and
        then let it happen – because it will – just allow!

"Today is a good day because I have the consciousness
        that can create it that way.
"I can solve and resolve any problem or situation so that
        the outcome is good for me. "
"So, I expect benevolence – I expect only good things to
        happen – this I decree!"

There is another daily affirmation that also should be said
        twice daily, once in the morning and at day's end just be-
fore you go bed, you should request assistance from
        your guides, the angles, and the masters
to help you prevent soul fragmentation loss due to fear,
        trauma or disaster.

Diet – You should begin to make some changes in purifying
        your daily diet.
It's an ongoing practice: unpasteurized raw dairy, raw eggs,
        raw vegetables, fruits, unroasted, unsalted oils, nuts
and seeds, unheated honey, but cooked starches and
        legumes – try it. (If you can't get unpasteurized
milk, cream, butter and cheese,
        oh well, you'll have to make do with what your local super-
market stores sell.)

Breath Work and Exercise – daily do some breath work
        and exercise.
And exercise should include aerobic, resistance and
        yoga – why compromise?
The masters have always said that mastery of the breath
        is a key to a longer life instead
of the short lives and early deaths that the human race
        currently sees and with breath mastery none of these need
thwart your incarnation now in progress, but
        few have training in any of this.

The 2nd Level Intermediate Monthly Practices

Knowing that negative thoughts and emotions are the
        primary causes of disease and afflictions are very import-
ant ideas for life extenders to learn and avoiding the
        trauma and the drama associated with many of these will
prevent the major illnesses – diseases that the
        life extender can then spurn.

And working with the Perfections and Healers
        will help to steel your mind
into the positive, compassionate, helpful states
        that are of the life extending kind.

<u>The Perfections and Healers</u>

Weekly, it would be good to choose a perfection
        and a healer group to work upon.
For one week write down situations for each group
        to seek healing and perfection anon.
For <u>kindness, compassion</u> and <u>love</u> note where it
        is hard due to your judgments.
Put yourself in the shoes of others to develop an
        impartiality to them that makes sense.
Many people cannot <u>surrender</u> old behavior patterns
        due to their biases and prejudices.
Let yourself be <u>vulnerable</u> to new situations and
        relationships – and replace the 'I' with 'us.'
In our hurried world most of us suffer discord and lack
        <u>patience</u> due to life's daily demands,
But <u>compassion</u> and <u>concentration</u> can transform
        discordant thoughts as if by calming hands.
<u>Humor</u> and laughter are higher consciousness and
        laughter yoga can help with this.
Laughter yoga laughs at anything and cultivates
        <u>slowness to anger</u> that is hard to miss.

Wisdom is gained from employing past experience
        and can help to increase your <u>self-worth</u>. <u>Contentment</u>
and <u>equanimity</u> are key to cultivating
        <u>joyful effort</u> easiest when work has some mirth.

75

<u>Fasting and Life Extension</u>

Fasting is an ancient practice of the traditional immortals
        of old and it allows the body to shed toxins
purifying all body systems many fold and the life extension
        practitioner should now add the one-day a week fast, and
it should be enjoyed for its cleansing and not
        looked at as something to hurriedly get past.

The 3ʳᵈ Level Intermediate Quarterly Practices

Many other factors play into this process of aging
      as the years unfold.
There is a death hormone that is activated that
      triggers aging – mankind's lot.
There is the low DNA's efficiency that keeps greater
      longevity on hold.
There is low stem cell utilization – it's longevity
      potential is not taught.
There is soul fragmentation which depletes life force
      energy causing aging.
There are past memories from trauma and drama
      that block love from engaging.
These need healing so that all humans can feel wanted
      and not insignificant.
Energy exercises and meditations can help heal –
      doing them is time well spent.
There is shimmering – a new tool for adding energy
      and for organ revitalization
There is the magic of sound for retrieving soul
      fragments and body regeneration
It would be good to do them in a quarterly cycle
      when you are starting out.
After you have mastered them, they will then become
      you without a doubt.
In all of these exercises, state your intention of what
      it is you want to achieve
And then bring in your guides, the masters and the
      angles, and allow and believe.

Mastering Halting the Death Hormone Release

You should know that you have a primal energy field
      that is in your DNA.
And even with a severed spinal cord it still connects
      to each and every body part it – carries signals

to and from your lungs, liver, kidneys, brain and heart.
          Your primal energy field (your merkaba) in your
DNA has a clock in each and every cell, and when millions
          of these clocks strike the same hour of your maturity, they
all signal the release of the death hormone –
          as birds signal others in their flocks – and then
your aging cycle really begins – but speech and intent can
          slow these parallels.
When your cells release the death hormone, this is key
          to when your aging program really steps in,
but here is an energy exercise that you can use to allow
          your life extension to win.

Assume a meditative position and create a scene
          of just one of your body's cells,
with your physical body and your primal energy field
          in it as if all were seen together in a dream.
It is important for you to know that your thoughts
          and intentions can override
any existing program or programs you don't prefer –
          these they can override and push aside.

These are the three aspects of your body that you will
          need to work with and engage.
Your primal energy field, your cells, and your whole
          body as a 'we-ness.'
Now when you speak to these three it is literally possible
          to set the stage for your life extension and rejuvenation
cycle to activate and express.
          You will speak in a low voice the intent of the lines
below and know that this will start to reverse
          your aging in a manner real, but slow.

"My primal energy field, as my friend, please listen up,
          I have for you an important task.
"Please disconnect from your magnetic short life imprint
          it does not serve – this is what I ask!

"Primal energy field, I choose to disconnect from your
          magnetic short life imprint - please heed my voice.
"It serves not. I choose an extended life –
          it is my desire and my choice!

"My cells, I instruct you to halt your death hormone release
          and deactivate your body clock.
"I am on a path of spiritual awakening – they do not serve –
          these I instruct you to block!"

"My body, we are in this as a team, and together we will
          heal all of our parts and our pieces.
"And choose to move into our contract as a life extension
          way shower.

"Together we three have power over the body clock –
          and the death hormone releases. "
"I request that these be dropped so that their affect goes
          away or is very much lower."

Again, speak to your team of three with words like these in a low
          voice –

"My primal energy field and my cells and my body, I decree
          that we as a team of three to hear and heed
my speech and know that my intent to bend my reality into
          the life of a life extender, indeed! "

"Death hormone release – halt!
"Body clock – deactivate!
"Long life – allow!"

<u>Adding Life Force Energy with Shimmering</u>

Shimmering is a new tool you can use to increase
          your vibration and add Chi.
Chi is life force energy and it can replenish soul loss
          energy to some degree.

In shimmering you visualize your auric field as a giant
        egg that encloses you
and shimmer or pulse this egg – make it smaller, then
        larger in a rhythm set to
A spoken tone such as this slow tone:
        ta….ta…..ta…..ta…..ta…..ta…..ta…..ta.
Then shimmer it faster, to a faster beat of your own:
        ta…ta…ta…ta…ta…ta…ta…ta…ta…ta…ta.
Then faster – your shimmer rate is your fastest known:
        ta.ta.ta.ta.ta.ta.ta.ta.ta.ta.ta.ta.ta
Shimmering will help keep your aura from developing
        a fissure, hole or crack.
Important for life extension because it prevents loss of chi
        which will set you back.

<u>Shimmering to Add Chi (Life Force Energy)</u>

Visualize a brilliant white chapel, you are inside,
        it is pulsing with golden white light.
The light pulses, pulses, pulses, you shimmer,
        shimmer, shimmer, and are one with the light.
You shimmer at an increasing rate, ta.ta.ta, feel the chi
        infusing you – you are becoming so bright!
Intend that this added chi repair and regenerate you
        all during the day and the night.

<u>Water Shimmering</u>

When you are near water and the sun shines and
        flickers and shimmers upon it,
breathe into the moment and shimmer with the
        Shimmering water and work on it.
Feel the life force energy flowing in and make an
        intention on how you will use it.
Sent it to your body parts that most needs healing –
        and with this chi infuse it.

<u>Breathing in a Column of Light</u>

While doing pranayama breath work an advanced
          practice is to breathe in light.
During the inhale, visualize a column of light
          streaming down - it is very bright.
Visualize it entering through your crown chakra,
          feel it flowing down to your toes.
Feel a bounce as it reflects back – and then into
          your energy meridians it goes.
During the exhale, visualize toxins as black specks
          flowing out with the breath.
They create aging - removing them puts you very
          far away from early death.
In this exercise, a slow precise rhythm or cadence is
          important to maintain.
The inhale-exhale timing should be constant to the ten
          thousandths of a second.
Inhale light in, exhale toxins out – your breath cadence
          is the best you can reckon.
After five minutes or so, intend this chi energy flow
          be used for healing,
and organ regeneration and body rejuvenation or
          whatever else is appealing.

<u>Massage Removes Trauma and Adds Chi</u>

Massage is a traditional way of removing past life and
          this life trauma
which occupies space in your cells and blocks chi from
          it due to the drama.
Deep tissue massage can bring to the surface and release
          this negative energy.
And this lets chi re-enter that space allowing you a higher
          light synergy.

Loss Retrieval from Disappointment

Visualize a spiral of light that is going up from the
          earth to the universe.
Visualize your guides, the angles, and ascended
          masters nearby and immerse
yourself in it – become one with it – breathe into
          this visualization and ask
that your soul loss from disappointment be
          returned to you and task
yourself with intuiting that your soul fragments have
          come back to you.
Periodically do this for 3-days – new abilities will be
          yours – let them accrue.

Soul Loss Retrieval from Fear

When you feel you have lost soul fragments from
          great fear or stress,
With a stick or stones or sand make a circle that
          surrounds you more or less.
Then make a Star of David inside the circle –
          stand in the middle and breathe
from the ground – ask your guides, masters and
          angles to help your soul sheathe
recover its lost soul fragments that have gone into
          nature –.do this for five minutes,
and when new abilities return and surprise you,
          know you have reversed traditional limits.

Full Moon Soul Loss Retrieval from Intense Emotions

The moon works with the water in your body and
          during full moons you can retrieve
some soul fragments – light a candle, hold a white
          cloth in both palms and weave

a beautiful light from the moon into your highest
        chakra high above your head down
into your lowest chakra beneath your feet and then
        request that soul fragments lost due to
intense emotional issues be returned to you and
        restored to your gorgeous soul gown.

<u>Soul Loss Retrieval with Sound</u>

Ancient sounds and mudras can call forth lost soul
        fragments because they put
you in resonance with the Earth – it brings fast healing
        energy – especially if barefoot.
The Sanskrit sound 'Aum' (not 'Om') opens meridians –
        earths and yours.
Toning this for 5-minutes or more can return lost soul
        fragments like water pours.
Tone "aum...aum...aum...aum...aum..." – and find that
        earth's resonance and yours are crossed.
Ask your guides, the angles and masters to help – and
        sense soul fragments returning that were lost.
The Hebrew sound 'Aurr' when toned with a mudra is
        very powerful indeed.
Your oversoul can link to multidimensional and solar,
        and universal levels and feed
you these higher frequencies (and soul fragments) and
        into your body they will come.
The mudra – point your index finger, wrap your middle
        finger around it, your other fingers touch thumb. Move this
hand position up and down between your
        mouth and third eye and say
"Aurr...aurr...aurr...aurr...aurr…" – and sense soul
        fragments returning from far away.

The 4ᵗʰ Level Advanced Yearly Practices

Indeed, it is possible to live far beyond 200 years like the
masters of old.
But you will need to be open to advanced practices like
these I am told.

<u>Poem On Activating Higher DNA Efficiency</u>

In our day for most people, their DNA is working at
only one third of its potential.
It is not well linked to their primal energy field or to
their body – only to what is essential.
But with higher DNA efficiency – greater linking –
a leap in longevity is possible.
Life extension students should work on this to convert
the impossible to possible.
The first thing to work on is to evolve into a higher level
of consciousness.
Work with the perfections and the healers and compassion
and suppress
The sub-human state which seeks power, wealth, and
domination at any cost.
For in the sub-human, a greater connection to the primal
energy field is lost.

The masters of old who did have their DNA working at a
much higher efficiency
All had a strong connection to the earth and her lifeforms –
and now this is now a deficiency.
Begin working with the earth – the animals, the plants,
all life that dwells upon her.
Communicate with earth – feel love for all creatures with
wings, scales, fins and fur.
Know that with higher DNA efficiency your body cells
replicate from stem cells

not from existing cells that replicate less and less
        accurately as aging tells.
Next, we will use our intention to request a higher efficiency
        level for our DNA.
As always, bring in your guides, the masters and the
        angles and then say,
"I request that my DNA efficiency be increased to the
        next higher level possible for me,"
and then allow it and expect an increase that you can
        notice will happen, and then just let it be.

<u>Poem on Becoming the Future Human</u>

In the future humans' day, ten generations, (200 years)
        past twenty twelve
futurists say humans will be living 200 years, so it would
        be good to delve
into their day and learn what they do that allows them to
        live that long
and emulate them – it helps us know that we, as life
        extenders certainly do belong.
The first thing that they do every morning is to say their
        daily affirmations

You should say them too – every day and let them
        become your daily life extension foundations.

"I am a life extender–life extension is calling to me.
"I intend to extend my life – I can bend realty and let it be."

The second thing is that they practice compassionate
        action whenever a suitable situation calls
They send compassionate action to help those whose life
        has taken a bad turn and falls.
Without getting involved, they send a powerful visualization
        that things will get better
to he or she who they see traumatized – future humans do
        this as a begetter

of better times, and indeed this action at a distance does
        set the stage
for better times and this compassionate action helps the
        victim to disengage.
And for the life extender it is a vital enlightenment practice
        and should be one
of the future human practices that should be incorporated
        by you and one that should be done.

The third thing, very different from our time now, is that
        their ego is very much less.
They are able to feel the joy and feel happy for others when
        others receive some success,
or something that they also wanted – we are far to "I"
        centered to allow that now.
But it's very wise for the life extender to work on "we-ness"
        and let it be and allow.

The fourth thing that they have developed is their intuition
        to a very high degree.
In situations with two choices, they ask their intuition for the
        best choice, do you see?
In a sense they tap into their own future self and this is
        something that you and I can do too.
You as a life extender should begin to do this until it
        becomes second nature for you.

The fifth thing they do is to redefine what today is called
        bad news.
In their day they rapidly redefined it as some change is
        coming their way.
And since they create every day to be a good day, they
        know that they can't lose.
Whatever it is, they know that the coming change will be
        something good anyway.
And so, they don't fret or worry about what we would call
        bad news.

And you as a life extender can see it as change and refrain
        from labeling news as bad – just refuse.

<u>Poem on Blocking Bad Memories from Past Traumas</u>

A frightening memory from a severe trauma may
        create a sleepless night
because it tends to keep you in the low vibration
        of fear and constant fright
and this takes an intolerable toll on your overall
        well-being and longevity.
As a life extender – of bad past memories and traumas
        you will need to be free.
They keep bubbling up, I know, but if you work on
        ridding them religiously
they will eventually fad away and no longer haunt
        you night and day.
Ask your guides, the angles, and the masters to help
        send them away.
These memories are stored in your body, your DNA,
        and in your mind.
The bad ones you want to block and replace with your
        good memories of a loving kind.

<u>Poem on Youthing</u>

Pick a day or a week in your future when you
        will choose to youth
and as the day draws near get excited about it –
        involve all of your helpers – don't be aloof.
Bring in the masters, the angles, and your guides –
        ask them to help you youth and be healed.
To youth, visualize just one cell, your whole body,
        and your primal energy field.
Image this one cell, instruct it to youth – you're the
        boss, it will do as you say.

Your cells are all connected, that one is linked to
        all the others, they all will obey.
Now, as a friend, speak to your primal energy field
        and tell it you want to youth.
Ask it to reverse aging and to rejuvenate all of you
        from thumb to toe to tooth.
Talk to your body, tell it, "We are going to youth" –
        expect results, slow but sure.
Results will come, but it is important that your thoughts
        remain steadfast and pure.
Next begin to allow a new playfulness to come in,
        playing, smiling, laughing –
for this sets the stage for your youthing to begin –
        and then let a new curiosity branch out –
get excited about life and all there is to learn –
        create a burning desire to know more
then before about what creates your new youthing.

Then allow it, expect it, and become impeccable about it
        in your day-to-day expectations.
You cannot vacillate – forget mainstream beliefs – let
        youthing become one of your new foundations.
Afterwards, once in a while, just smile to acknowledge your
        youthing with a knowing and a nod of your head.
This reinforces your expectancy and allows some aging
        to shed with youthing instead.

Poem on the Long-Fast

Ah yes, the long-fast was a major technique as
        used by the masters of old
to live several hundred years, creating an
        immortality of sorts we are told.
Of course, this will not appeal to many of you,
        but it can be done – it is there.

I have done a long-fast four years in a row now,
        and you do get used to it; this I swear.
I define the long fast as one that runs anywhere
        from one to two months.
Before trying it, you should first read up on it, but
        after doing it even only once
you will find that it is do-able, but I must add that if
        any long-fast mishaps should occur
I won't be held responsible, read the contras,
        and know the contra-indications as it were.
But I personally have had no negative effects from
        doing my long-fasts – I am a fan.
It removes toxins and death hormone cells better
        than any other practice can.
In the long fast you are to consume no solid food at all,
        but you must have water.
You can also have a small amount of vegetable or
        fruit juice as a meal spotter.
Surprisingly, after the fourth day you will not feel
        hungry – your body will begin to feed
it's vital organs with disassembled substances –
        you will not starve indeed!
Studies on two groups of worms: one continually fed,
        the other continually fed-fasted
have been done and repeated with the same results
        that the fed-fasted group outlasted
the continually fed group by seventeen times – they
        lived seventeen times longer!
I have done long-fasts of 4, 5, 6, and 7 weeks now –
        one every year –
and afterwards, my body is always more vital with
        health issues healed and I'm stronger.
What are you willing to give up to live to live much
        longer than one hundred years?
As a life extender, how far are you willing to go to live
        several hundred years? What are your fears?

<u>Poem on Sexuality</u>

Studies show that expressing your sexuality can
      increase your longevity.
Indeed. it can lengthen your life and negate to some
      degree the status quo brevity.
You should know that your birthright is to delight
      in the dance of the night.
It is good to accept that it is a delight to savor and
      relish the dance of the night.
There are even those who say that closest one can
      come to The Infinite Creator of the All
is in the orgasmic experience – and in the East there
      even are those who teach
that in aftermath of man's long journey into decent
      separation, warfare and fall –
that man will evolve and rise to savor the moments
      of the clouds and the rain
to experience the pleasure and ecstasy of creation
      and do it over and over again.

<u>Poem on Developing Mastery</u>

Many years ago, I was told by a master teacher I studied
      with that I was a master.
Three times he said it, "You are a master! You are a
      master! You are a master!"
Those words sunk in, I do have resolve, I do the processes,
      and the results I achieve.
As the master from Galilee said, "What I can do, you can
      do also," – this I firmly believe!
Let me say unto you, "You can be a master! You can be a
      master. You can be a master too!"
And you can, you can decree that you are going to extend
      your life – mastery for you!

Reactions on an Advertised Trip to Meet the Immortals

"Count me in," said Hank the Finn,
Let's go and meet the immortals
And seek the immortal portal
And push beyond what's ever been before
On the western shore and open wide the door
Of the unlimited abilities and potentials of man,
And go where only the bold and daring can!

Memories From a Trip Advertised as, "Meet the Immortals"

A trip, a trip – there are immortals you can meet!
Far away, far away – immortals you can see and greet!
In India, in India – it's only half a world away.
Immortals are there, go now – and don't delay.
Come along, come along – and don't say no.
I went, expectant; I could hardly wait to go.

But, once there, doubts about the trip began to
        surface thereabouts.
The trip was a disorganized dichotomy of immortal
        ins and outs.

The first week saw those who had come to see
        immortal join in
the daily routine – reading immortality affirmations –
        a small token
of the real reason of why they had come – to see
        a real human immortal,
one who had lived far longer than the rest of us and
        learn from them from words spoken.
The days, the hours of the first week slowly came
        and went.
Rupees, rickshaws, rebirthing, Hindu Temples,
        monies spent.
Climbs up holy Girnar Hill, heavy traffic, horn's
        a'honking, holy cows,
women in saris, weddings, Indian couples exchanging
        marriage vows.

The second week saw more seekers, the curious, and
        a camera crew,
Indian cuisine, lion preserves, Gugarati names
        pronounceable to only a few,

curious boys, coconuts, monkeys in trees, sacred temples,
	red forehead dots,
the Shivratri Festival, Junagadh, naked Naga Babas
	smeared in holy ashy blots.

The third week's attendance of the 'Meeting of the
	Immortals' soared to sixty strong.
All come to see immortals – hundreds of years old –
	surely, all of them could not be wrong.

But as the days went by, one by one, no immortals
	were seen, not one –
no immortals at all. But surely, they must come to
	the Shivratri Grand Parade –
come to our beck and call – and as the great parade
	drew near, so too did our excitement,
as did our fear.

We were excited that we might see them, but we
	feared that we might not, and these two went
back and forth as if they fought, at this Grand Parade
	immortal premiere.
Pilgrims packed the holy grounds at the Shivratri Festival
	Grand Parade Finale –
orange-robed priests, temples at night illuminated in light,
	loud speakers rally.
The parade began, children's bands, the naked Naga
	Baba, temples in carts. monks in orange,
Hindu floats, Junagadh dignitaries, Naga Baba
	private parts.
"He is immortal – one hundred ten," said one pointing to a
	frail, white-haired saint. "
Merely long lived," I scoffed, but in the deafening din no
	one heard my complaint.
The parade procession, an endless stream went on and on
	until midnight.

A pandemonium of the Naga Baba and a TV crew jostled
        for the holy site.
Naga Baba by the dozen jumped into the holy waters to
        become one with Shiva light.
And then it was over, and no immortals were seen or heard
        or had come that night.

And so, when the next day dawned, disappointment was to
        be our lot.
We had come to India to see 'The Immortals' and see them
        we did not.

Chapter 3, Poems on Rejuvenation

Ode to Ambrosia

To C.A. Gage, 2017

Someone said, "At times, he likes to use his middle name." "Yes,"
they claimed, and his middle name was Ambrose. Later, after
Ambrose and I had met, I brought up the same. And lo! to me he
explained, "It means Ambrosia."
"Ambrosia!" I exclaimed. "The food of the gods
      which became
Their secret to immortality. (And here, I upstarted
      and arose!)

Aghast, I was astonished, and I said, "Your middle name is
      linked to the god's – and to their immortality –
and I too am linked to it too – against all odds!"

Agog, I wanted to know more and I google searched
      the word.
And I found many myths of Mount Olympus and the
      gods of Greece.
Ambrosia – the god's food for immortality – this it
      conferred.
Ambrosia – is found in many myths, unlike Jason and
      the Golden Fleece.
From Hera's lovely face, all defilement it cast away –
      this it spurred.
From Penelope's aged body, it erased her aging and it
      did this with ease.
And restored her body to such sultriness that her suitors
      she could tease.
Athena gave it to the hero Heracles to grant him his
      immortality.
But refused Tydeus – human brain eater – this gift.
      How could he?

Awestruck, I was about these ancient Grecian gods, but
          yet I wonder
about a huge archway in Tiahuanaco and all around it
          are hieroglyphs
carved in stone and they may cast asunder notions
          of immortal gods –
perhaps they were merely mortal men who had found
          or made
an ambrosia – an elixir – to reverse aging – and the
          Greeks blunder into making myths of them as immortal
men, ageless without bound, when perhaps
          they were merely mortal men advanced in sciences and,
in technology which we too can learn and use to
          escape from aging – with its struggle, stress and trouble to
emerge younger and engaging!

In a sense, I too am linked to the gods – for one
          and twenty emails
outlining a rejuvenation technology – a process to reverse
          aging – were sent to me – from an extraterrestrial source
– with all the details.

Three steps to rejuvenation in a language cryptic
          and engaging.
Emails having all the hallmarks of exotic and exciting
          future tales.
Step one – a regenerative energy streaming that
          sets the staging for
step two – the consumption of a very special
          elixir smoothie, and
step three – vibrational and magnetic – such as in a
          special effects movie.

Well, let it be – let us return now to immortality – and that
          stone archway and query, "What do those stone glyphs do
up there?" And, "Why did all attempts to
          translate them fail?"

It wasn't known then that the message wasn't for
        primitive man.
Great care and wisdom was in it – it was meant for
        the ET visitors alone
to help primitive man evolve – it was a hieroglyphic
        message prayer given to those advance ET visitors from,
a constellation Draco star – tall, peaceful, three-
        fingered hands – not how earth men are.

And from many star systems far and near have these ET
        visitors come and gone.
Lauded as legendary immortal gods either imperious
        or nefarious.
They've come from the Pleiades and done men much
        good or wrong.
Or they've come from other star systems: Orion, Vega,
        or Sirius,
or from Andromeda, or Zeta Reticula,
        (Oh, I could go on and on)
or from Thiaoouba or Essassani or the whole Universe
        (Here, I get delirious).
And after many eons have elapsed these ETs either
        evolve upwards into unity
or downwards into warfare and annihilate themselves
        without impunity.

Agape, I stand with all of this as I imagine ambrosia
        granting immortality.
I sing to those ancient immortal Grecian gods and of
        how they could beguile.
I know the ingredients for ambrosia which I can receive
        as payment for a fee.
I will ingest ambrosia to see if it can grant immortality to me
        – ah, but let's wait awhile.
I know that rejuvenation requires three steps and ambrosia
        is but one of three

steps to reversing aging – but if it works – I swear I will
    wear the biggest smile!
And so, I salute Ambrose whose middle name is linked
    to the gods –
And to their immortality – and I swear I am in it too –
    against all odds!

Rejuvenation Devices Are Coming

In 1998, there were futurist who planted a seed
And said, "Indeed, rejuvenation will come for the need."
When and what and where, only spirit knows.
But I tell you this – of the builders – I am one of those.
Slow in coming, they will appear all around the world.
The banner for extended life spans has been unfurled.
So, keep your course strong and steady as she goes.
Even if it storms and a tempest wind blows.
Soon the devices will be ready for the shows.

Lines on a Past Life

To V. Tunnerman, 2002

Ah, the poems you send me try
To awaken the immortal cry
That lies many layers deep
Within the soul I keep.
Thousands of years ago
Before the ice and snow
In a legendary land you know
As Atlantis, I was there.
A machinery commander rare
In charge of devices used
To treat the aged, old abused
And return to youth and bloom
Those soon to reach the tomb.
That memory of long ago
Prods me now to reinvent the show.

Lines on Rejuvenation Devices

A dream of long ago
Slowly began to grow
As devices of rare design
Sprung from the human mind
Took form in shape and view
To rebuild the body anew.

As the years came and went
And a portion of youth was spent
So, too, the devices grew
In size and shape they were two.

There comes a time eminent
Of the testing on lady and gent.
Will they work or no.
Will it be weal or woe?

Only time will tell
But at the ringing of the bell
And they are turned on...well.

Will the devices boom and thunder?
Will they flash and smash asunder – aging?
Well, at this time we can only wait and wonder.

Rejuvenation Devices – The Beginnings

It began as an eddying about a concept
       as in a dream.
An inspiration (or other brilliance)
       as it may seem.
Most light a little hour and then
       they are gone.
But this one stayed and lingered
       and lasted long.
It grew and spread and soon
       became a plan.
To build rejuvenation devices for
       woman and man.
These devices were seen as into
       vision grown
to restore to womanhood, she
       who was a crone,
and to manhood, he who was aged
       and skin and bone.
The structures slowly seemed to solidify
       on my mental screen
and they slowly separated into three
       precious visions seen.

First there was sound which did abound with
       resonate power all around
vibrating organs, tissues, bones in
       a crescendo surround.
Sound chambers slowly solidified
       into sold form
to manifest a life span that might
       exceed the norm.

The second was magnetics and legends
        from ancient times.
The Temple of Rejuvenation re-emerged
        from ancient designs,
to repolarize human tissues into their
        primal magnetic template state
which in legends rejuvenated humans so as
        to bypass the aging fate.

The third is a gift from extraterrestrials to
        help the human race
conquer aging—Natas Rejuvenation may
        restore maturity—and aging erase.
It uses regenerative energy, an elixir, and
        a magnetic field with vibration
to add new stem cells and re-energize and
        re-polarize for a longer continuation.

When the timing is right, all three of these devices
        will be developed and pursued.
Many more methods will surface to rejuvenate
        the body and keep it youthful and renewed.
Indeed, the beginning of rejuvenation is coming
        and will be here in a few decades—soon.
And so current wisdom says, it is wise to plan for
        the future and not for the tomb.

Rejuvenation and Many Things

The time has come the walrus said (of 2019 to 2022)
        to speak of many things:
of the shutdown that COVID-19 brings,
        and of the rejuvenation that Highman sings,
and what is meant by Black Lives Matter,
        and what do the demonstrations,
vaccinations, storms and heat, fires, and wars do to
        stir the pot, so that humanity rises to the
higher consciousness of a unified people who will
        welcome rejuvenation and the re-making
of a world that embraces more benevolence and
        much more care taking,
such that the homeless have homes, the elders and
        the weak are included
and taken care of, and all are happy and seek longer
        lives, and when the human debts are satisfied
and give place and human race meets
        its galactic cousins
face to face (instead of only seeing their stars
        in the night skies)
and hears about their very long lives –
        well, then we too will want to pursue
and develop the many ways our bodies can be
        revitalized, and we too will want rejuvenation
to live twenty thousand more days to experience life
        extension's ways and to claim a body that
doesn't die but stays.

Rejuvenation in Atlantis

I cannot lose the image from my mind
Th story that unfolds is both supreme and sublime
What glories arise out of yesteryear's that have come and gone?
Temples of Rejuvenation and Regeneration – the image lingers on.
Ghostly scenes from ancient times seem to float within the air.
Giant crystals and majestic temples pop up everywhere.
Cities with domes of light in great beauty glow in green and red
Cloned genetic human mutants not of women bred.
Legends of them work in the fields and farm,
Or in the factory or in the military arm.

Amazing tunnels underground connecting all continents to the whole
A floating crystal city played and important – then later – deadly role.
Tall humans with legendary life spans that never seem to end
Oppose others immersed in a more malevolent bend
This was ancient Atlantis that now seems to come back to life.
Will it show us a legacy of destruction within its olden strife?
Or within the glory of its legendary stage
Will it lead us into another golden age?

Rejuvenation and the Cleaning Woman

"Why, Gina, only yesterday you was so old and bleak.
"I just want my rejuv," was all you'd sigh and speak.
"An now you got your rejuv, and now you're young and pert.
"An ever since your rejuv, you ain't no more like dirt.
"An all the men 'round you, say you're such a spoiled flirt."

"I wish my own life could be half as excitin' as yours,
"Instead of havin" no fun and havin' to scrub the floors.
"Instead of never havin' 'nough money, n'never endin' chores.
"I wish I could be young n'pretty again like you, you see,
"An be a bloomin' beauty with all o'the men a'chasin' after me."

"Why my dear, you can't have that," said Gina,
"Cause you ain't been rejuv'd yet," said she.

The Rejuvenated River of Life

Oh, the river of life flows on and on
Once you've been rejuvenated
The river of life is long, it's long
When you've been rejuvenated.
Oh, they'll be time enough for love's
           sweet song
For the song of love goes on and on
           once you've been rejuvenated.

The Joy of a New Atlantis Rejuv

Oh-ho-ho, we're off to another rejuv,that we go,
     we go.
Ring-a-ding-ding, does it not just make your heart
     Want to sing?
Oh, so blest, won't you please come with me to see
     and be my guest.
Eee-yi-yo, Atlantis rejuvenation was quite complex
     you know.
Ta-ta-tone, of the many processes used, one was
     indeed, a major cornerstone –
It was 'The Temple of Rejuvenation' – and it had a large
     turntable as its central station –
and there was a large cone above and one below – one
     cone reached high; and one cone hung low.
The cones held the two magnetic engines and do what
     only magnetics can do –
they repolarized and rebalanced the body's organs back
     as if totally remade anew.
Gong! When turntable spins – and the magnetics are on –
     bong, it's equals rejuv's song.
So now we know that it's off to the turntable that
     the old one goes.
Spin-spin-spin, now we see the turntable floor slowly
     begin to spin
around and around upon its pin the turntable floor
     slowly begins its spin.
And mounted off to the side is the target table –
     it is like a cot or a very narrow bed
and the old one is on it – and horizontal to vertical
     goes the old one's head.

The target table swings up and down and rotates
        round and round.
It's mapped to go round and pivot up and down –
        with the old one strapped Inside –
rotation within rotation inside magnetics –
        for a real rejuv ride!

But know that in Atlantis, rejuv was complex – as
        revealed by those who wrote articles
about it from blocks of thought from the higher realms –
        and they were taught
and shown other steps for healing and regeneration
        used in Atlantis Rejuvenation.
Other techniques utilized biochemical and biogenetic slavs
        and injection
to regenerate teeth, hair, bones, glands and organs to
        restorative perfection.

And healing from periodic exposure to trace levels of
        slightly radioactive radon gas wasused.
In our times much fear revolves around radiation but let
        us not get confused.
Radon health spa literature reveals that in trace levels,
        radiation is healing and its use is appealing.

Rare deposits of a special living mineral were found
        and mined and consumed.
Crystals (some very large containing trace amounts of
        gold) were roomed in large octagonal temples
above and below ground where the rejuv was resumed.

Phi-cut crystals help humans maintain their concentration
        to a high degree.

In Atlantis they were used to perfect the power of the
        mind to hold and see
their major organs restored back into perfect form with
        removal of all toxins and debris.

And so, oh-ho-ho, after the rejuv there was a party with,
        Oh, so much joy and celebration.
And so, sing along sing, and a special robe was worn to
        bring sacredness into the occasion.
And now, oh so blest, the old one – much younger now –
        was wondrous with joyous elation.

When I'm Newly Rejuvenated

When I'm Newly Rejuvenated
I will always have a love of life.
When I'm Newly Rejuvenated
I will rid myself of hate and strife.
When I'm Newly Rejuvenated
My life goes ever on and on.
When I'm Newly Rejuvenated
My life from age-to-age travels on and on.

Geraldine's Rejuvenation

I sing, I sing of Geraldine's Rejuvenation for
It will bring, it will bring her a whole new spring
And ring, and ring in many, many more new years
And end the sting, the sting of all her aging fears.

The Rejuvenator's Song

Well, we were a rejuvenation crew, we had a machine
       or two and we knew exactly what to do to renew
our clients back to prime of life.

Our rejuvenation fame with the old, with the lame, our
       clients they came with an application and a name, waited
just the same, with hopes running high, and most
       were man and wife.

But one day we had a woman come from the slum and she
       certainly wanted some rejuvenation done, and she didn't
want to wait.

We diagnosed her heart, made a chart, did our part for the
       paper work to start, but it put us in a state.
We wanted to decline, it was time to toe the bottom line,
       but she proffered us some wine and we had to hesitate.

Well, we had a heart of gold, she was old, very bold, we
       wanted her rejuv to unfold, her youth to recreate.
So, we gave the certain brew, an elixir which we knew
       could undo her worn bodily form and renew it back to
seventeen.

We strapped her to the table, she was able, she was
       stable, her rejuv would be no fable, so we started the
machine.

The table and floor did begin to spin round the pin and
       within the tumult and the din there was a mild uproar. She
went spinning round and round, table rose
       and tilted down, magnetics all around, she was a clown
and hollered out for more.

The magnetic field, it came on, it was strong, like a
        rejuvenation song resonating all along her aged DNA in a
most repolarizing way. The magnetic field was
        a sword, did afford her aged DNA a new accord
in which her youthfulness was restored within the span of
        a day.

The machine, we let it run, it was fun, our aged client was
        no nun, and we said, "We ain't done, we've got several
more steps in store for you!"

So, we tested her for sound, made a round, found
        imbalance all around, gave corrective frequencies
of sound, it was a song for her body to renew.

Then we coached her in the ways to extend her days, enter
        the immortal phase to the surprise and amaze of all the
friends that she knew.

We had a robe and mask for her to wear, protect her skin
        and hair, and I declare gave her more elixir rare before we
took her to the next machine.

We strapped her to the seat to repeat her rejuv with a real
        youthing treat so her results could be so sweet that she
could pass for seventeen.

The new machine, we turned it on, it vibrated all along,
        played her song, lightening flashed all around, her new
rujuv began to dawn, began to spawn, she was being
        annealed.

The tubes, they did begin to flash, seemed to smash, the
        lightning bolts they did lash, a flood of light seemed to
stream and crash, peeled the shadows from her energy
        field.

Then it was done, but there was one more fun thing that we
wanted to do for her rejuvenation scene.
It was the feast, not the least, she won't soon be among the
deceased, see her rejuvenation sheen!
Now all is done, we had great fun, our lady's had a wild
run, now all salute our new rejuvenation queen!

Simple Simon Learns About Immortality

Simple Simon got a dream from Highman
       while he was pondering radon healing.
Says Highman to Simple Simon in his dreaming
       "Thirty more years are possible with it," –
in telepathic word-thought communication streaming.

Simple Simon read about co-joined mouse arteries
       in one minute –
It said the old mouse got young, but the young
       mouse got old.
Says Highman to Simple Simon, "Old blood has
       aging factors in it –
if old blood is replaced with new blood, age reversal
       can unfold."

Simple Simon heard about ancient immortality
       and wondered if they lied –
when yoga masters said they lived several
       hundred years.
Says Highman to Simple Simon, "Periodically
       they purified –
primal diet, breath work, and the long fast, all
       anathema to your peers.

Simple Simon heard about new ways to live longer –
       senolitics, biogenitics, biosubstances and more.
Says Highman to Simple Simon, "They may help you live
       longer and these you can explore."

Simple Simon heard about the ancient's higher
       consciousness and wondered if longevity was
a part of it.

Says Highman to Simple Simon, "They would bless –
        mother earth and nature and meditate with
candles lit.

Simple Simon got a vision sent from Highman
        while he was going to a retreat.
Says Highman's vision to Simple Simon,
        "The Temple of Rejuvenation equaled three
lifespans in Atlantis – three, oh so sweet."

The Highman sent Simple Simon an email message
        while he typed gibberish upon his computer.
Says Highman's email to Simple Simon,
        "Natas Rejuvenation can do sir!"
Says Simple Simon to the Highman,
        "We got an email from Natas one night
and we wish to know more when the timing is right."

Says Highman to Simple Simon,
        "Natas has accepted you.
"Your rejuvenation can come true,
        "if all his steps you follow through."

Highman Returns

After seven long years during 2008, Highman returned
And had much to share and much have I learned.
Highman called me Ardigee, and thus bestowed upon me,
Rejuvenation device builder to some degree.
Highman said that crickets have a precious gift to give.
The chirp of rejuvenation – with a longer life to live.

Ode on the Red White Elixir

"Oh, of menstrual blood and semen – do not speak!"
Say the prime and proper – "Such things reek!
Of incivility, impropriety and taboo!"
What – immortality might exist within that brew?

"Oh, of congenial conversation it makes a breach,
"Speak no more of it the meek beseech."
But has not the race of man been steered away
From all that could and can make death delay?
Do not men and women close their eyes to kiss?
Whereas with open eyes there is a soul-to-soul bliss.

"Oh, the insolence of it – not another word
"About this horrid mix – it is simply absurd!"
So, mock the dubious and doubtful herd.
"I simply will not hear of it." say some
"Even if it could put aging on the run!"

Yet, a boon issues forth from underneath the belly.
Ah, the seminal fluid of man, ah yes, the jelly.
The white (male derived) – the primordial seed
When mixed with the red (woman bled) can indeed
Set the stage for the immortality of man
And woman when ingested as part of the plan
Of rejuvenation – this red-white elixir is the brew
The second of three steps to rejuvenation for the few
Who can overcome the pettiness and piety of their peers
And undergo rejuvenation when the door of death nears
And triple the span of the number of their years!

Ice and Flapping and Immortality

Ice and flapping
Lots of chanting
Singing for the soul

Now, the ice has to do
And this is certainly true
With you and your permanence.
Just as the ice stays frozen in form
And does not decay, wear down or go away –
Like a glacier – frozen ice is here to stay.
Can you not keep your bodily form on ice,
By perfecting yourself to keep aging at bay?
Can this not become your way, day after day
To keep yourself away from physical decay?
Now wouldn't that be nice? Does this suffice?

Now, let us speak about the flapping
It is linked to Poe's raven's rapping
And tapping on our chamber door
Bringing sadness and fear forevermore
This vampires our will to keep on going
And blocks our life energy from flowing.
Can we not chant and sing immortality verse
And flap to scare away the evil vampire curse
To reach a sort of immortality bye and bye
And live on and on and on and not die?

Do this always
For all the days
You will reach your goal.

Perfection is immortality
Immortality is perfection
This is what you know
That is all you need to know.

Reprogramming Your Subconscious for Life Extension

We should acknowledge the great discrepancy
Between longevity's potential and what we see.
We should choose not sadness but a sort of glee
In letting the masses live short lives while we
Choose to use longevity's tools to become free
From premature aging – and we note that the seed
For short lives is planted in beliefs and programs that feed
Instructions to curtail regeneration – we can be freed
From this to some degree in meditation by connecting
To our past selves – 1, 5, 10, 20 years ago and injecting
Love and longevity – repeat for our future self – affecting
Them deeply, and re-programming our present for long life
Thereby re-directing our present self for life extension
Deflecting aging for an immortality of sorts – and let me
mention – this helps to create permanence by perfecting.

Your Later Years Can Be Your Best

Your later years can be your best.
So why not let them be
And savor them deliciously?
Why would you cut them short?
And let your later years abort,
When there is so much to see and do
And learn and know and grow into?

Why not pass longevity's test
And live to see your later years
Without health or personal fears
Long life gives you time enough to do
Everything you've ever wanted to.
It lets you see what the future will bring
Let your golden years have their spring.

Why not live to see the rest,
And reap the rewards of life extension's test?
By 2070 – a world primarily at peace -
Rejuvenation appears – lifespans increase.
By 2100 – humanity has become
Unified – the whole more important than the one.
By 2130 – our galactic cousins befriend
We roam the galaxy! We evolve! We ascend!

To live on to see your later years – this is the quest
Of he or she or him or her who seeks longevity
Without a frail, fragile, feeble body that is the guest
of today's old – of this decrepitude, decree to be free.

The early aging human of today is surely not your way.
Life extenders regenerate themselves for a longer stay.
And after a hundred and twenty years have come and gone
They still will look maturely youthful and keep on going on.

Taoist Immortality

Oh, immortality is in the here and now
For those who follow in the ways of the Tao,
And others who learn the sanguinary ways
Of adding a century or more to the span of days.
Can these poems assist you for a year or more?
And help you take charge and cast off from the shore
Of the land where fear reigns king and a human ages?
Where it grips and grabs with a hard hand even for the sages.
Can you sail the seas of the immortality of a woman and a man
And forge a new brotherhood of the budding immortal clan?
Oh, you have read my poems, but have you truly heard?
Is an immortality of sorts in your future, or is it somewhat blurred?

Epilogue

Oh, poets of yesteryear have eulogized lives
       that were harsh and short.
Long lives full of creativity and sweetness
       I extol and I wish to escort
Mankind's short lives (the way of it 'till now)
       to that which has had its time
In this little book of mine that sings of
       longevity in verse and rhyme.
And if you resonate to this idea and goal
       of a longer lifetime,
Why not take steps in that direction while
       there is yet time?
I have outlined the basic path that the life extender
       must take.
But it is always up to you to climb longevity's
       hilltop and to partake.

Oh, men and women have always lived
       short lives up until now.
The time is ripe to reverse this,
       but the major problem isn't how –
It is that humanity will continue on
       with short lives and won't allow
Their natural long-life spans to flourish and so
       your goal will be
To let them be as they may while day by day
       you choose to be free
Of premature aging and early death – and
       this takes a very strong will,
And a strong character to pursue the path
       of life extension and longevity

While all about you, others create their short life
      and blab about life's brevity.
Indeed, not an easy journey – it would be good
      for you to add a little levity
Along with an indomitable determination to
      manifest your own extended longevity.

Bibliography

Deng, MING-Dao, The Wandering Taoist, San Francisco: Harper & Row, !986

Michle, Gregor, Roxanne Cox, and Allan Watson, Pranayana the Breath of Yoga, Doubleview W.A.: Kalvalya Publications, 2012.

Orr, Leonard, Physical Immortality: The Science of Everlasting Life, Chico, CA: Inspiration Unoiversity, 1991.

Shelton, Herbert, Fast and Grow Young, Hygientic System VolIII, Dr Shelton's Health School, San Antonio, TX, 1934.

Shelton, Herbert, Fasting Can Save Your Life, National Hygiene Press, 1964-1981.

Vonderplanitz, Aajonus, We Want to Live: The Priimal Diet, Santa Monica, CA: Carnelian Bay Castle Press, 1997.

Vonderplanitz, Aajonus, Recipe for Living without Disease, Santa Monica, CA: Carnelian Bay Castle Press, 1997.

Life Extension Products, www.lifeextension.com

People Unlimited, www.peopleunlimitedinc.com

RAAD Fest, www.raadfest.com, annual age reversal conference

Sedona Journal of Emergence, www.Sedonajournal. com, articles revealing new life extension techniques, 1998 - 2020.

The Church of Perpetual Life, www.churchofperpetuallife.org